Uprise

ADVANCE PRAISE FOR *UPRISE*

"How do we cope or get the very best out of ourselves in everyday life? Resilience? Grit? In *Uprise* Kevin addresses these issues in a way that helps bring the reader to not only believe in themselves, but to put into practice the art of mindful self talk that creates positive mental Drive. In *Uprise* Kevin helps us get the very best version of ourselves."

Casey Fannin
~Three-time Xterra World Champion, International Triathlon Union World Champion, Off-Road Triathlon National Champion, and Multiple Time IRONMAN Triathlon Finisher

"As an experienced teacher, coach, author, and educational consultant, Kevin is well positioned to share his expertise in helping others build their powers of resilience. His compelling writing style is accessible, and his recommendations are consistent with correlations from neurocognitive science research. He provides strategies, compellingly revealed by examples, to sustain motivated effort even after setbacks. He also emphasizes how we can all help others 'redirect their viewpoints.' What wonderful opportunities he presents to 'Provide the uprising lifts for others to develop minds primed for growth, performance, and achievement.'"

Judy Willis
~Neurologist, Teacher, Expert in the Neuroscience of Learning, and Best-selling Author

"Kevin has written a true masterpiece when it comes to developing 'grit' in our everyday lives. We can spend a lifetime physically preparing for something, but our attempts can be unsuccessful if we don't develop dogged determination and grit. Kevin gives practical steps on how to win the mental game and extend our capacity to endure when life throws a curve ball or when circumstances get tough and aren't going in our favor."

Travis M. Sherman
~Multiple Time IRONMAN Triathlon Finisher
and IRONMAN All World Athlete

"We've all faced setbacks in the past and will experience many more in the future. Kevin Washburn's book, *Uprise*, is a must-read on mindset and provides hope to help us rise up and move forward no matter what comes our way! We were made for so much more. It's time for us all to become 'uprisers.'"

Zac Bauermaster
~Educational Leader, Principal, Speaker,
and Author of *Leading With a Humble Heart*

"Kevin's writing and clarity gives me the focus to tackle the challenges that we all have in life. His insights on personal problem solving and introspection will inspire you to rethink the obstacles that have been holding you back. Success is never easy, but Kevin's succinct writing will provide you with the mental roadmap you need to achieve your goals."

Jack Jacobs
~Attorney, runner in training

"With relatable examples and engaging anecdotes, Kevin walks the reader along the pathway to resilience, clearly defining (and redefining) the goal and the attainable skill set needed for the journey."

Erica Speegle
~ U.S. Olympic Marathon Trials Qualifier,
Certified Running Coach, and Mother

"Kevin Washburn provides readers with food for their soul, elucidating psychology research through the use of stories and anecdotes that hit close to home. *Uprise* is an accessible read for those striving to achieve new goals, increase resilience, and influence others. I highly recommend it!"

Matt Townsley
~Educational Leadership Professor and Author

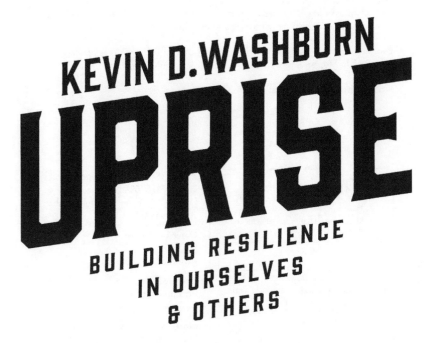

KEVIN D. WASHBURN

UPRISE

BUILDING RESILIENCE
IN OURSELVES
& OTHERS

NEW YORK

LONDON • NASHVILLE • MELBOURNE • VANCOUVER

Uprise

Building Resilience in Ourselves and Others

© 2024 Kevin D. Washburn

Published in New York, New York, by Morgan James Publishing. Morgan James is a trademark of Morgan James, LLC. www.MorganJamesPublishing.com

Proudly distributed by Publishers Group West®

ISBN 9781636982984 paperback
ISBN 9781636982991 ebook
Library of Congress Control Number:
2023949432

Cover Design by:
Rachel Lopez
www.r2cdesign.com

Interior Design by:
Christopher Kirk
www.GFSstudio.com

Illustration in Introduction and Photograph in Conclusion by:
Julia S. Washburn

Edited by:
John Paine

Morgan James is a proud partner of Habitat for Humanity Peninsula and Greater Williamsburg. Partners in building since 2006.

Get involved today! Visit: www.morgan-james-publishing.com/giving-back

*For Greg, who taught me how something as simple (and serious!)
as fun can pull people together, lift their spirits, and help them achieve
the impossible. I still miss you every day, my friend.
And for Jack, who won't let me quit.*

CONTENTS

INTRODUCTION

*Failure is simply the opportunity to begin again,
this time more intelligently.*
— Henry Ford

*uprise: verb • to rise up, move forward, mount up
Example: I will uprise and try again with a better plan.*

The body cannot outperform the mind. Achievement cannot outpace the mind. Relationships cannot outgrow the mind. For every area of your life—the goals you have, the dreams you envision—your mind plays an indispensable role. And it's your mind that, more than anything else, enables you to uprise.

We do not get to choose the brains we are born with, but we can choose our mindsets. We can view ourselves and the world through the lens of hope or the lens of defeat. We can dig deep and persevere, or we can quit. Mindset determines the moment-to-moment decisions we make—decisions that can add up to rising strength.

Our mindset supports or undermines developing grit and resilience. This connection isn't always clear. For years I attended conferences where one researcher would share findings from studies on mindset. Another would introduce research on grit. A third would present conclusions about resilience. Each time I kept asking myself the same question: Why aren't these researchers talking to one another?

The three topics seemed to me more like campsite companions than lone hikers. Wouldn't mindset play a role in grit? Doesn't grit overlap with resilience? Isn't mindset as important after success as it is after failure? The questions piled up until I tried to find answers. I developed diagrams, attempting to identify how the concepts could lead to results. Then an additional question emerged. With a hat tip to Tina Turner, "What's hope got to do with it?" Finally, the relationships became evident. The model on the next page reveals how hope, mindset, grit, and resilience work together.

It also reveals the contrast between how a person uses the present and past to address the future. Looking to the future with belief and curiosity fosters resilience and renewed effort. Regarding the future with fear and pessimism fosters surrender. The way we look at what we've done in the past can help us find the perspective we need to make progress.

As we approach a new stage, we need a mindset that is willing to learn. Whether we are tackling a new sport, changing our diet, or starting a new job, we have to believe we can improve through effort. We need a positive vision of what can be as we start working to make that vision our reality. We need grit to pursue the immediate next steps to gain us the result. When we experience setbacks, we need resilience. We have to use the challenge as a springboard for growth rather than a reason to quit.

UPRISE Model
The Learning Mindset — Grit—Resilience Connection

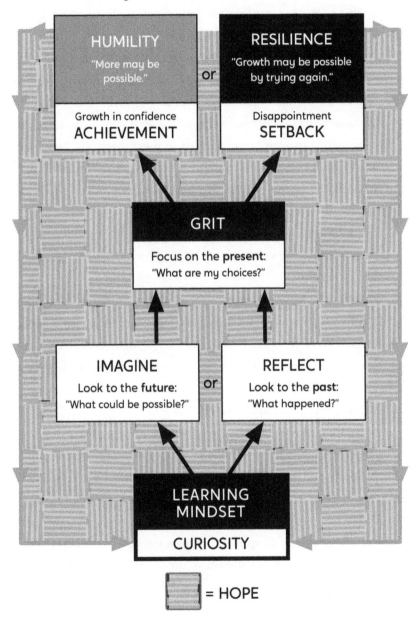

HUMILITY
"More may be possible."

Growth in confidence
ACHIEVEMENT

or

RESILIENCE
"Growth may be possible by trying again."

Disappointment
SETBACK

GRIT
Focus on the **present**:
"What are my choices?"

IMAGINE
Look to the **future**:
"What could be possible?"

or

REFLECT
Look to the **past**:
"What happened?"

LEARNING MINDSET
CURIOSITY

= HOPE

All of these productive mindsets share a foundation. They are built from a base of hope. Hope looks ahead, excited by a possibility and willing to work toward it. The yoga practitioner who tries a new position requiring exceptional balance must hope to master the stance even when early attempts end in falling. The parent working with a child on math homework must hope that the instruction enables learning of the concepts and skills. The lawyer seeking to become a partner must hope that her work rises to the level of quality and attention that merit the promotion. In each of these scenarios, hope does not sit idly by and wish for things to happen. It considers the potential and strives to make it reality. And when setbacks inevitably happen, hope knows they are temporary.

Think in terms of the adverb *yet*. I cannot hold that position *yet*. You cannot solve this math problem *yet*. I am not a partner *yet*. Failure is only final when you quit. Hope is the fuel of uprising.

We tend to overlook hope as one of the three main virtues, along with faith and love, that should characterize our lives. Love is the greatest of them, but James Evans, a pastor/writer friend of mine, points out that hope is what makes the influence of both faith and love possible. Without hope, we may be able to possess faith and love, but we will squelch the influence of both.[1]

Hope also requires humility. You have to grant yourself the grace to make errors and develop a strategy for improvement. For example, an athlete will review film to identify areas that could be strengthened. A businessperson will review a recent interaction with a client, looking for ways to more clearly communicate ideas. A scientist will welcome feedback as they continue to refine a project. Endlessly curious, the learning mindset chases sustained improvement rather than mere moments of glory. You want to stay in it for the long run, not just the dash to the finish.

At the start of a challenge we need two things: (1) a vision of the end of our efforts, and (2) the belief that we can make progress toward that vision. If we lack vision, we will lack direction. If we lack belief, we will struggle with motivation. The danger is focusing on one without a connection to the other.

Kendra, for example, has a vision for her pottery. She dreams of having it exhibited in art museums. When she eyes the lopsided bowl sitting on her wheel, one of two things will happen. Kendra may allow impatience to spark negative thoughts: "I can't even make a basic bowl. I'll never be good enough to get something into a museum!" In her mind, she has disconnected the present from her future vision. She has not recognized the effort she will give from now to then. She has left out the development that needs to happen between the current misshapen bowl and the future work of art.

Alternatively, Kendra may eye the bowl and think: "Okay, this is not beautiful, not even functional. Let me figure out why and then consider how the next bowl can be better. I'm not ready for the museum yet, but I can improve my skills with some reflection and a strategy. I can make a better bowl tomorrow." With this perspective, Kendra connects her vision with the steps she can take now.

When we have a setback, as Kendra with her wonky bowl, we need to inject hope. A learning mindset focuses first on the past. What did we try? What prevented us from being successful? What changes can we make in strategy before trying again? Then, with what Henry Ford described as beginning again "more intelligently," we work toward our vision once more. To get started, look ahead. A vision will give you direction, motivation, and hope. To start again, look back and figure out what went wrong. Then renew working toward your vision. Look ahead, try, look back, try again—that is the pattern of achievement.

With her healthy mindset, Kendra can begin to work, and so can we. The steps we make and the actions we take happen in the present. And even with vision and belief, things can get challenging. That's when we need to find the willingness to continue giving the effort. We need to find grit.

Grit has nothing to do with tense jaw muscles, but the grinding of teeth is often celebrated. We think the determination on a speed skater's face pushes her to that needed 100th of a second. Or the clenched jaw of a father enables him to address the school board emphatically. Or the steely focus of the medical student will enable her to ace the anatomy exam. Yet by the time a person shows their grit, they have already had it for some time. Grit is not suddenly discovered in a moment of need. The groundwork for that determination was laid well before the event. That established groundwork gives us better options when the chips are down.

Grit is a mental tool we need to practice. In our pursuit of physical goals, professional progress, and relational growth, we will encounter challenges. These challenges can spark doubt. We consider putting up a white flag. Quitting seems inevitable. We can meet these challenges with mental fortitude if we have developed grit. Building such resolve enables us to direct our thoughts toward triumph at the moments when success hangs in the balance. We can train to overcome. We can learn to uprise and meet challenges with smarter effort.

A recent day started with my usual morning routine, which included inserting my contact lenses. When I stuck one into my left eye, I knew after a few blinks that something was wrong. Somehow I had torn the lens. I became more aware of my limited vision. If I looked to the left or right, things were unclear. Straight ahead, all was well. It felt like tunnel vision. Seeing anything clearly required moving my entire head in that direction.

Resilience is like that: where you look. Specifically, about where you direct your thoughts after a setback. It's easy to resign yourself to disappointment. Failure generates feelings that can override positive thoughts. It takes more effort to see new possibilities. But we have to choose to turn toward a mindset that will guide us to success. Resilience is not available to a select few; we all can be more resilient than we are today. We can come back from setbacks. We can alter the trajectories of our careers. We can repair relationships. We can be uprisers.

However, resilience does not grow by looking in a mirror and saying, "I am resilient." It is developed through practice. Challenges can drive us to think negatively when we need to focus on what is working for us. Defeat can make us want to go it alone when we need the support of close friends. Setbacks can cause us to ignore the very information we need to improve. Hindrances can cause us to be morose when we need humor. Adversity sets plenty of traps, but by practicing resilience, we can avert them and advance toward our goals.

But let's be real: we all fall into emotional funks. Sometimes a setback seems so overwhelming that we can't help but focus on our failures. The playoff game was lost by one goal, and you were the team's goalie. The conversation with the potential client went off the rails, and they signed with your competitor. The professor made a decision that negatively impacted the outcome without any chance for an appeal. The conversation with your estranged adult son only deepened the division. These are difficult challenges, and they can cause us to stew in disappointment for days.

When trying again seems like too much to ask, we can dig our way back to hope by facing the feelings head on. They are legitimate, and they motivate us if we approach them the right way. Rather than forgetting them and turning away, we need to examine them for significance.

Exploring our disappointments for changes we can make or for meaningful insights can convert failure into fuel for uprising. How do we search for meaning? Writing is one way to slow down, explore what happened, and brainstorm paths for further progress. Getting together with the right kind of friends—those who will empathize but also challenge us—can help us process circumstances and yank us out of a pit of dismay. Changes in scenery can lead to changes in outlook. Or, simply listening to music can reverse a downward spiral.

Similarly, learning something new can provide fresh vantage points from which to examine the past and strategize for the future. Returning to an activity we love, even if it's where we failed, can be restorative if we do so without expectations. Perhaps the most powerful tool is practicing the Golden Rule. Doing for others breaks us out of focusing on ourselves, provides us with newfound meaning for our actions, and enables us to move beyond self-pity.

And while you rub elbows with others, you can help them become more resilient too. Teachers can help students find resilience. Coaches can help athletes bounce back from defeat. Parents can help their children thrive through times of challenge. And friends can help each other plan ways to move forward. Such a powerful impact starts with understanding what others are facing. We need to know a scenario well enough to give advice that will be beneficial. Where we encourage others to "look" can influence their mindsets and enable them to find resilience. The more resilience we encounter in our environment, the more we ourselves are likely to develop resilience. Yes, we can change our worlds!

In Part 1, we will lay the critical foundation of hope and explore its connections to mindset and grit. In Part 2, we will cover resilience, including strategies for increasing its influence on our efforts and character. Finally, in Part 3 we will consider how we can help others develop resilience.

If, like me, you want more than the status quo, you need to become an upriser. Maybe you want a healthier life or to try out something you've never done before. Maybe you want to do the same thing faster or better or for a more noble purpose. Maybe you tried and failed but still want to succeed. Maybe you want to accomplish something without people knowing or with everyone knowing you are working on it. Maybe you want more friends or deeper relationships or, yes, a better world.

Growth and change are possible. If you yearn for more than what your life currently offers, you need a resilient mind, one that acknowledges that failure only happens when you quit trying. You need a mind that uprises rather than quits.

Let's get started!

PART ONE
GROUNDWORK

CHAPTER 1

HOPE: STARTING AND PROGRESSING

*Hope can arrive only when you recognize that there are real
options and that you have genuine choices. Hope can flourish
only when you believe that what you do can make a difference,
that your actions can bring a future different from the present.*
— Jerome Groopman

I was more than halfway to the finish line when a headwind took
everything out of me. I was done. I didn't care that I spent months
training to run the race. I didn't care that the pace group I had been
running with might notice I was missing. I didn't care that I would
have to tell my family that I had quit. I wanted out. Now.

I stepped off the Richmond marathon course and asked a sympa-
thetic-looking spectator to please call my wife. She handed me her cell
phone and told me I could call.

"Hello."

"Honey, it's me. I'm just done. Please come find me and get me out of this."

"Are you sure?"

"Yes. I just want to be anywhere else. I'll keep walking until you find me."

I handed the phone back to its owner, thanked her, and began dragging myself in the direction others were running. They were headed for the fun and glory of a finish line. I was not. The phone call only finalized what I was feeling inside.

Contrast this to a race I had few months later. I found myself sitting at a counter with my head resting on my arms. Cincinnati's pre-marathon expo had zapped all of my energy. What I had tried denying for three days was now unavoidable: I was sick. My wife took me to an urgent care facility that was open on a Saturday afternoon.

An hour and an injection later, we headed back to the hotel. I slept the rest of the afternoon, ate a little supper, then slept until the morning. I felt good at the start of the marathon, and for eighteen miles, the shot worked its magic. I kept my target pace and was headed toward a personal record. And then the injection wore off, which the doctor had indicated might happen. Again, I found a spectator who graciously handed me his cell phone.

"Hello."

"Honey, it's me. I'm fine, but I'm not moving very quickly. However, I want to finish."

"Are you sure?"

"Yes. This race is known for being fun, so my goal is to have as much fun in the next eight miles as possible. See you at the finish."

I felt as bad as I had in Richmond, perhaps worse, but I found a reason to continue. No personal record would be set that day, but

I still look back on that race as a victory. I finished when the going got tough. And, yes, I laughed multiple times in the remaining miles thanks to the creative distractions the Flying Pig Marathon's organizers and volunteers provided.

The body cannot outperform the mind. Yet you do not have to run a race to know that. This holds true across every endeavor we try. What is telling us we can't jump the next hurdle?

For Marion that hurdle was office politics. She frequently found herself on the losing side of disagreements and felt like she lacked an advocate among her colleagues. Speaking her mind had always been one of her "strengths." Personnel issues in the office became personal, and Marion made decisions defensively, saying things without thinking through their potential effects.

When her boss approached her about an idea she had proposed, Marion braced for combat. The boss said she liked the idea and wanted to refine it for possible implementation. Marion took a breath and prepared to defend the details of her proposal. But in a moment of inspiration, Marion realized her reaction would likely result in the entire idea being discarded. Hope infused her thinking; maybe the idea had potential! She took a forward-leaning step and said, "Great. How can we revise this so that it is beneficial for the company?" After thirty minutes of conversation, the idea had been improved, even by Marion's standards.

Accepting criticism and refining ideas became a practice that Marion's colleagues noticed and welcomed. After a while Marion's boss considered how she could expand Marion's realm of influence within the office. A career that had reached a plateau now possessed an upward trajectory.

Relationships cannot outgrow the mind, either. So much of what we do involves others. So even if you are making progress toward a goal, people are always throwing up obstacles. How you handle them determines whether you are stopped in your tracks or not.

Derek taught high school math. Students knew he had high expectations, but he would make sure to equip them to successfully tackle problems. He was respected, and students loved his sense of humor. Young adults who usually shied away from advanced mathematics took his classes. His classroom was a positive, challenging, and safe environment.

One parent, however, found fault. His child was not earning the highest grades in Derek's class, and he was convinced the teacher was to blame. Derek listened to the parent and then showed the father evidence of the student's lack of effort. The parent was unconvinced and dissatisfied. After stomping out of Derek's classroom, he went straight to the vice principal. Following that meeting, he arranged one with the principal. And then the superintendent. Derek found himself defending his teaching methods over and over. The superintendent arranged a meeting with Derek and the disgruntled dad.

As Derek prepared to once again defend his approach, he started wondering about the parent's motivation. Was he out to get Derek? That didn't seem likely. Derek knew of no reason he would be targeted other than the student's lack of achievement. Derek began reviewing what he knew about the student and her father.

He remembered that a tragic car accident a few months earlier had left the dad a single parent. He recently had begun working second shift at the police department, significantly limiting his waking hours with his daughter. Derek realized that his approach, while justified, was unlikely to resolve the problem. He had to find another way to help this student succeed.

At the meeting, he responded to the dad's objections by offering assistance. "How can I help you help your daughter be successful?"

The dad, taken aback by the kind offer, paused a moment. He then asked if Derek would be willing to assist his daughter in developing a checklist for assignments—a list of the tasks that needed to be completed with deadlines. That would provide the dad with an understanding of his daughter's progress (or lack of it) at a glance. Derek eagerly agreed, and the dad stood up, shook his hand, and thanked him repeatedly.

The disgruntled dad became Derek's biggest supporter. When he sought funding for his students' entry into a math tournament, the dad lobbied the school board on Derek's behalf. What was contention became cooperation.

We love such rebound stories. They remind us that we have to adjust to the setbacks life deals us. They inspire us to work harder to improve our situation. And they give us reason—beyond mere victory—to cheer.

However, we often view the protagonists of such stories as if they are made of different stuff than mere mortals.

We learn that a bus accident dislocated a Mexican woman's spine and left her in a lifetime of chronic pain—before she became a world-renowned artist. Right, we sigh, but I'm no Frida Kahlo.

We learn about a shark attack that stole a surfer's arm, but she kept surfing her way to major championships. That is an inspiring story, we agree, but I'm not Bethany Hamilton.

He was rejected by 27 publishers before finally getting his first book published. Yeah, but I'm in no way Theodor Geisel—a.k.a., Dr. Seuss.

All of them must come from another planet where resilience is part of the aliens' DNA.

We know none of this is true, but it's more comfortable to live with excuses than to see ourselves as capable of such mental and emotional strength. Yet you know that such stories stir something inside of you. A seed of potential whispers, "You can be resilient too."

And that whisper is right.

A Practical Type of Hope

Every step forward begins with the thought that something good can happen. During his initial presidential campaign, Barack Obama suggested his administration would bring change to the United States. An artist's rendering of Obama with the word *hope* inscribed below it became widely distributed—and frequently mocked. Sarah Palin referred to this slogan as the "hopey changey thing," as if hope were nothing more than an ephemeral emotion with no real potential for influence.

Politics aside, she disparaged the very thing growth requires.

Hope does not have to be merely an emotion. Those with the courage to hope are not passive, waiting with fingers crossed for things to magically improve. Hopeful people work to make a vision reality.

Hope can:
- carefully consider possible futures
- develop and act on plans likely to move the vision closer to reality
- keep its eyes open, adjusting plans and work as needed.

In addition, hope:
- is not surprised but delighted by positive outcomes
- knows that setbacks and discouragement are temporary
- recognizes failure as an opportunity to learn, adjust, and keep working
- is not fragile but can be both lost or bolstered.

As a child you may have been told to "dream big." The sentiment is on target. We need to envision possibilities beyond our current constraints to perform up to our potential and grow meaningful relationships. However, hope is not wildly unrealistic in its focus.

For example, Darnell dreamed of opening a restaurant, but her resources were limited. Renting a space, redecorating it, and hiring the necessary help entailed expenses she could not afford.

One morning over coffee with a friend, Darnell shared her dream and frustrations. Her friend listened empathetically and then said, "Have you thought about catering from your own home? I know it's not a restaurant, but it would give you a way to share your cooking with others." Darnell had not considered anything other than the elusive dream of restaurant ownership. She researched her friend's idea. The licensing costs and needed changes to her home kitchen were within her budget. These were investments she could make without risking her life savings.

Within a few months Darnell launched her catering business. The restaurant dream still remains, but she has found a path that she can go down and enjoy in the meantime. The mind empowers achievement. Through hoping for a *possible* future, Darnell found a way to start living her dream now.

Hope plus action increases the likelihood of success, but there are no guarantees. Still, even when one's goal is not achieved, hope rarely lacks benefits. Darnell may never own a restaurant, but working for it will make her a better chef and equip her with additional financial and social skills.

You want to place your hopes on a challenging objective, an endeavor that will require real effort, but keep it to the realm of the possible. Wishing on a star is fine, but how will you ever get there? Wishes lack the power to sustain continued effort. You are destined to fall short of the ultimate vision if you don't achieve victories along the way. Disappointment chews away at motivation because you feel like you are working without making any progress. Focus your hope on both the short term and the long term.

The ability to shift your perspective really matters. Here is a simple illustration of how directing your long-term sights affects results. A rest area in central New York state doubles as a scenic overlook. You pull off the highway, and after you park your car, you can look in all four directions. Take a quarter turn to the left and you will see a few unremarkable trees. Another quarter turn and you're staring at I-81 South. One more quarter turn and you'll face the building housing the bathrooms. Where the heck is the scenic overlook? In one more quarter turn you can behold the majesty of rolling hills, open spaces, and river valleys. Sure, you are surrounded by the pedestrian walks of life. You just have to find the view that makes you feel uplifted.

Here is a similar analogy that can help you as you set off on your way. My wife, who grew up in upstate New York, used Lake Ontario, one of the Great Lakes, as her reference point. She navigated her hometown in relation to that body of water. Is the city library toward the lake or away from it? The lake kept her from getting lost. She framed her location and directions according to its relationship to "the lake."

Hope is like that. It helps frame your outlook, and it helps you navigate your steps toward your objective.

One doesn't work without the other. Hope needs a viewpoint that looks forward with both intention and reasonable confidence. Turn one direction just a bit and you see wishing. (I hope I get a check for a million dollars in the mail tomorrow.) Turn the other just a bit and you see short-lived desire. (I hope this rain clears before we get to the park.) Hope—real hope—casts its eyes to the future with purpose and belief.

Back when epistles were the email of their day, the Apostle Paul emphasized this connection: We strive because we hope. The statement does not include a guarantee. There are always other factors that influence outcomes. But you won't strive in the first place unless you have hope.

Develop Plans

For years Gabe dreamed of writing a book. While in college, he wrote a short story for one of his classes. The plot stuck with him. He spent a lot of time exploring possibilities for expanding the conflict into a novel. His wish for the book to be published popped up while spending time on other activities. Between episodes of the TV show he was currently binging, he dreamed of the few years he'd spend writing. During karaoke night, he wished he could add "author" to his resume. While crawling in afternoon rush-hour traffic, Gabe imagined his story appearing on the shelves of his local bookstore.

During a conversation with friends, someone asked a question: "One wish. What do you use it for?" Immediately, Gabe called out, "To write a book!" His friends, intrigued by this sudden response, asked more questions. Do you have an idea for a book? Have you tried writing it? How long have you wanted to do this? Why haven't you tried yet? Gabe answered each question, but his doubts about what he was doing didn't end when the conversation shifted to another topic.

Gabe couldn't get it out of his head. Why was he just wishing? The story was in his head. With a few changes in priorities he could make the time available to write. Could he hope to get the words down on a page? Eighteen months later, Gabe began submitting completed manuscripts to publishers. Hope for an attainable object of desire led to accomplishment.

But as Gabe discovered, looking forward with intent means developing plans. It is not vague, it is not directionless, it is not denying reality. With hope must come planning. And that planning primes the mind for action.

When President John F. Kennedy stood before Congress in 1961, only three years had elapsed since the Soviet Union's launch of *Sputnik* sparked the Space Race. NASA was hardly old enough to go to preschool. Yet here was JFK proclaiming, "I believe that this nation should commit itself to achieving the goal, before this decade is out, of landing a man on the Moon and returning him safely to Earth." The goal was so audacious that one MIT mathematician dubbed it a "moondoggle."

In 1969, Neil Armstrong made the first boot prints on the moon's surface. In between, NASA did a lot of planning. Learning led to failures and further learning. Man didn't magically materialize on the moon. A goal supported by rolling cascades of planning made the "one small step" possible.

Most people don't have an entire government agency working for them, of course. Yet we see them succeed every day. A sculptor, Jody hoped to get one of her works into the nearby art museum's annual exhibition. For three years straight she sculpted, submitted, and her work was rejected. As she began contemplating another year's entry, she paused. She had collected the exhibit guides from each year, and she studied the works of all finalists featured in them. She recognized a pattern: all of them were conceptual in nature. The sculptures portrayed ideas rather than literal objects. The judges for this competition preferred such artworks. With this new knowledge, Jody began to carve in a purposeful fashion. This time her finished artwork made the cut. Hope plus a plan landed her sculpture in the exhibition.

Your ambitions don't have to be so lofty. You can make changes that affect your everyday life. Take Eric, for instance, standing between his refrigerator's opened doors, staring at its contents. As his eye fell on the maple syrup, he remembered the chocolate frozen waffles in the freezer below. "Yes!" he thought. And then a conversation he'd had earlier came to mind.

His doctor had suggested that he lose some weight. The results of recent bloodwork showed Eric could soon need medications for diabetes. He sighed deeply, knowing the doctor was right. Suddenly, nothing in his refrigerator looked appealing. He wanted to lose the weight, but he was still hungry. He closed the refrigerator, took a deep breath, and said aloud, "Okay, I'm going to have to plan a way I can eat something."

Eric began researching. Soon, he found recipes for easy, healthy meals he could make ahead on the weekend and eat through the week. He found snack ideas that sounded tasty. He started a shopping list, referring to the items on it as "Success Supplies." He set up a chart where he would record his weekly weight. For every pound lost, he would add a color-filled box to the chart, giving himself a quick visual representation of his progress.

A few weeks later, he discovered a "moving meditation" group in his area. Every Saturday morning he joined them on a walk or hike that included meditation breaks. He found the camaraderie motivating and the mindful pauses refreshing. At his next physical, his doctor remarked on his healthy weight, and the bloodwork raised no concerns. Eric had transformed himself. Hope, planning, and action moved him into the fit and healthy column.

It's not enough to just wish. Focus on an attainable future and plan your way there. If the moon is not out of reach, a little planning can likely transform your possible future into reality.

Eyes Open

Singer/songwriter Brian Doerksen has a terrific line in one of his songs: "Hold on, the light is breaking through. Don't close your eyes."[1]

Giving up is easy when a task becomes challenging. We rationalize our way into conceding defeat. Today is not my day. The weather is lousy. My back hurts. I didn't sleep well. The people who organized this event didn't set it up for me to be successful. My spouse is being unreasonable. My boss is biased.

Yep, we can find an excuse for every time we give up.

It's true that sometimes our performances are influenced by circumstances. Any runner who has tried to run in hot, humid conditions will tell you that despite the best training possible, the weather gets a vote. Same with the photographer who has one day to photograph a remarkable landscape but ends up with a flat tire that prevents her from catching the optimal natural light for the scene. And for the parent who unknowingly brought up a topic about which a teen is touchy.

But how we respond is our vote, and ours alone. As Aloe Blacc sings, "It ain't what happens to you, it's what you do about it."[2]

Think about the last time you gave up on something. How did you explain your decision to others? Quite likely, you invented an excuse and made it part of your story. This is how we talk ourselves into losing hope. We stop envisioning a possible future and quit making plans. We give ourselves permission to close our eyes.

You can see it all the time in the office, and not just for colleagues lacking confidence. Take Barrett prior to his annual review. He enters his supervisor's office, self-assured of his job performance and his qualifications for the available promotion. Things have been going well. All his important work statistics exceeded expectations. He was one of the first in the office every morning, and one of the last to leave in the afternoon. He knew this extra effort had been noticed because his boss recently mentioned it.

The conversation started as expected. Barrett's numbers were exemplary, and he was consistently in the top tier of monthly employee results. Then the word *however* was voiced. Barrett was occasionally rude to his colleagues. When possible, they requested to work on teams led by someone other than Barrett. He was quick to claim successes and equally quick to place blame. This inability to work positively with others argued against his promotion.

After scowling and wringing his hands for several minutes, Barrett turned away from the letdown and started thinking how he could do better in the future. A year from now, he determined, he would not be cited for this flaw. He set up new expectations for himself. Every Friday night he reviewed the past work week. Had he lived up to his aspirations? After falling short for a few weeks, Barrett decided some extra accountability might help. He arranged with a friend to meet for coffee and a chat once a month. Aware of Barrett's goals, the friend reviewed the month, week by week, with him. The plan began to yield results.

When he attained a success, Barrett now acknowledged his coworkers, making sure to mention that their hard work had led to winning a new client. He began encouraging colleagues to volunteer for his teams, listing the strengths each would bring to the project. His genuine interactions were noticed, and after a few months Barrett became a popular team leader. At his next review, the boss made not one comment about his negative relationships with colleagues. When the outcome was not what he wanted, Barrett looked for a plan that could change the result.

Hope perseveres, not by gritting your teeth and forcing something to happen, but with strategic thinking and a willingness to achieve more in your life.

You can use it for more than a future aspiration. When hoping for a better future, you loosen the binds that hold you to your everyday extreme. It helps you to become a bigger person, someone flexible enough to bend to changing circumstances.

This can have very practical results. I do a lot of public speaking, which means I often deal with less than ideal situations. I was teaching one time in a remote locale where the electricity was spotty. In the middle of my presentation, the power surged and the projector flashed brightly and began to smoke. All my handsome charts and photographs were now only visible to me. I paused the presentation. My display materials were out the window, and yet I still wished to impart my message to the audience.

I asked the person in charge if a chalkboard or white board was available. While I continued to teach, a cracked, small white board was located and placed in the front of the room. I kept going, using my subpar stick figure illustrations, in a room dimly lit by the room's three windows. Was it ideal? Definitely not. Did it work? Yes. Hope presses ahead even in less than ideal circumstances because it holds onto the possibility of a good outcome. Perfectionism can prevent positive results because you're more focused on how short you may fall rather than toward what remains possible.

When you're able to adapt, you can shape your hopes toward a backup plan that may work out even better than the original idea. For example, Karla hoped to win the lead role of the community theater's upcoming musical production. She prepared hard for the audition. She studied the character's lines, working out the emotion needed for each scene. She worked with a vocal coach on the song for her audition. Her presentation to the director was easily one of the best.

A few days later, Karla clicked open the email labeled "Audition Results." She did not win the lead role. The supporting role she got seemed like a setback. Still, Karla decided to move past the disappointment and help in another way to make the musical a success. She studied her assigned role as thoroughly as she had the lead part prior to the audition. She realized that her character's big music number was a showstopper, and that the role held great potential for humor.

She gathered a group of friends, explained that she was going to interact for 15 minutes as she believed her character would, and then jot down notes about what made the others laugh. This trial-and-error step paid off big-time. By opening night, Karla's castmates had become concerned they wouldn't be able to hold back from laughing in scenes they shared with her. She didn't steal the show, but the audience loved Karla's portrayal. Every evening the audience would rise to their feet for a standing ovation when Karla came out to take her bow. When her hopes failed to become reality, she regarded the disappointment as a sign to adapt. She didn't settle, she strategized. She turned her focus and energy toward what remained possible.

When the going gets tough, you must persevere, strategically. Don't close your eyes. Turn the light of hope toward the next goal that inspires you.

Summary

Hope is more than a feeling. It can be a battery—stored energy looking for the direction in which it should empower movement. Once that movement is ignited, hope keeps looking for what is possible. And as we'll see in the next chapter, hope responds to both success and setbacks.

Circumstances may diminish your happiness. They may make you question your determination. They may even make you doubt yourself and accept defeat. But, as you're already starting to see, there is never a good reason to give up on hope.

CHAPTER 2

HOPE: FALLING AND LEARNING

The very least you can do in your life is figure out what you hope for. And the most you can do is live inside that hope. Not admire it from a distance but live right in it, under its roof.
— Barbara Kingsolver

H ope is more than a starting line for our race toward possible futures. It also guides responses as we run the race, celebrating progress, recognizing setbacks as temporary, and guiding learning from failures. Since hope holds so much power, we need to guard it. We need to make choices that bolster rather than diminish our hopes. Let's examine these active characteristics of hope.

Delighted by Outcomes

Quite simply, hope celebrates.

You prepared for that presentation, you communicated clearly and smoothly, and you really engaged your audience. Sure, that second point could be strengthened with a better anecdote, but you could tell people considered your ideas. You shouldn't be surprised that things went well, but you should be delighted. Later you will review it all and further develop that second point, but for now, allow yourself to celebrate the elation.

That can be hard when you fail. Let's take a look at an extended example to show how a business owner faced an obstacle and then moved on, making better decisions afterward because of it. Alyssa was running her restaurant during a lunchtime rush when a customer came in, yelling accusations across the counter. He claimed that two weeks earlier he had been given the wrong milkshake, and the one he was given contained peanut butter. He bellowed that the error landed his young son, who has a peanut allergy, in the hospital waiting room. The boy ended up being fine, but the father had been stewing in anger for two weeks. Now he was letting loose with a large crowd listening.

Alyssa asked the father to join her at a table. She came out from behind the counter and sat down across from the angry man. He continued to rant, repeating things he had already said. His anger was like a virus he needed to spread, and everyone in the room felt ill witnessing the confrontation.

Alyssa gave the man her full attention. When his tirade had run its course, Alyssa responded. "Sir, I am very sorry for any mistakes that I or one of my team members made. And I am very sorry that you and your son had that terrifying experience. There is no way for us to make up for it." Alyssa continued, " I am going to meet with my team tomorrow and review the safety procedures, including communicating with customers about drinks that contain potential allergens. You have made us aware of a problem, and I will take steps to make sure it does not happen again." The man harrumphed.

Alyssa pressed ahead. "Now is there anything we can do to assure you we have addressed the issue or to make some amends with you and your family?"

The man did not reply right away. His body language suggested he was at last relaxing. However, he did not accept Alyssa's offer. In a calm voice he said, "No, nothing you can do. We will not be back. I think reviewing things with your staff sounds like a good step." He pushed away from the table and walked out the door.

At first Alyssa thought she had failed. A lost customer is never a good outcome, especially when his anger may have discouraged other customers from coming. Yet there was nothing she can do about him now. All she could do was influence the future.

The next morning, Alyssa led the team meeting. She started by providing drinks and pastries from the cafe next door. She wanted her team to feel good about their work. Then she explained the situation. They talked about reviewing customers' orders before handing milkshakes over to them. They shared strategies for dealing with irate customers. They role-played, practicing those strategies. At the end, the team thanked Alyssa. They felt good about their ability to work more effectively with their customers. Alyssa found a way to celebrate the team while enabling them with critical skills. A step forward to celebrate, even when the outcome was not what they hoped for.

I tell runners I coach that they should celebrate some aspect of every race. The race may not have gone well, but you didn't miss a single workout during the training cycle. Be delighted. You worked hard and came very close to your ideal finish time. Forget those few seconds by which you came up short, at least for now, and be delighted with what you did accomplish. You ran a great race but missed being in the top three of your age group by two spots. Hey, you were in the top five. Be delighted.

Failing to recognize progress can cause setbacks. A mistake as minor as a slip of the tongue can have lasting consequences unless you move to correct it. As you may know, saying you're sorry sometimes isn't enough. You have to keep working to make things right. This can happen even with people you know well. After an awkward conversation, Jerrid lamented his inability to completely smooth things over with a close friend. He should not have said what he did, the way he did. That one moment of poor judgment erected a wall between him and his friend. Although Jerrid dreaded making an apology and put it off for a couple of days, he finally accepted responsibility and asked if their friendship could return to its former state. Instead of welcoming the opportunity, his friend replied, "I'll think about it."

Jerid had created forward movement. He had sincerely apologized. Instead of finding contentment in that, he beat himself up for the original mistake. A day later, when his friend called and asked Jerrid to go rafting with him the following weekend, Jerrid was caught off guard. He had played out the worst possible outcomes over and over. It took him several moments to respond because his thoughts were still several steps back in the sequence of events. In his mind, the friendship was over because of his mistake. His friend stepped into the long pause: "It's fine if you don't want to. See you around." The phone line went dead.

If your response to every effort that comes up short is to beat yourself up, you are short-circuiting hope. Accumulated rounds of self-regret will knock you down and keep you down for the count. Don't do that. Let results delight you. Accumulated delight feels like progress, and progress motivates the search for new hope. For now, be delighted and celebrate. Reflection and revision come later, and hope influences those processes too.

Setbacks Are Temporary

If you try, you will likely fail before you succeed. This simple fact can be difficult to accept. How you view failure, though, significantly influences your capacity to be resilient. Those who see failure as fatal give up quickly. A child may strike out in one game, but if he is harshly reprimanded by a parent afterward, he will view that failure as fatal. A woman who equates not winning a contract because she is not good enough will view the failure as fatal. And the parent who thinks a relationship with his adult children is impossible to improve also views failure as fatal.

Failure is "fatal" when it prevents regrouping and trying again. You are ultimately unsuccessful only when you quit trying.

That doesn't mean that an unnaturally perky attitude or fake smile are the best response to setbacks. It's okay to feel the frustration of failure. It's not healthy to let that frustration overwhelm you. Feel it, but don't let it settle in your psyche.

How do you go about finding new fortitude? Let's consider Amir, who certainly felt the sting of defeat when he hung a "Going out of business" sign in his store window. Two years earlier, he had turned his passion for model railroads into a business that offered local train enthusiasts a place to find anything they needed for their locomotives, boxcars, and cabooses. Amir's store was not just a place where these hobbyists shopped; it's where they met to talk tracks with others.

Then the COVID epidemic hit. Amir had to shut down his store for several months. Even though the property owner had only charged half of the normal rent rate, it proved too much for the store's limited finances. In the meantime, local model railroaders found places online from which to order the latest models and pieces for their displays. There was no coming back. A week after the sign was hung, Amir was out of a job. His business had failed.

At first Amir felt grief over the loss. He moped. He grouched. He thought about getting a job he wouldn't like but that would pay the bills. He quit going to the local business council meetings, and skipped the next social held by the local railroaders club. He felt like everyone he saw was thinking the same thing: what a loser.

When the dust of disappointment cleared, Amir realized that the store had not been a wasted effort. He had introduced model railroading to younger generations. He had met new friends who shared his interests. He had strengthened his customer service skills and learned how to manage the finances of a small business.

Amir realized he now had a valuable skill set. "How could I turn those skills into an income?" he wondered. "And could those skills give me an opportunity to do something I enjoy?" He updated his profile on a social media site for professionals and changed his job status to "looking."

When a phone number popped up on his screen, he did not recognize it. "Probably spam," he thought, but at the last second he answered it. The woman on the other end explained that she was from a new company that created full sets of scenes for model railroaders. "For example," she explained, "instead of selling all the pieces needed to construct a model amusement park separately, we sell kits that features all the necessary pieces. We have kits based on the top five amusement parks in the world."

Amir responded that the idea sounded interesting, but that he was no longer running a store that sold such items. "I know," explained the woman. "That's why I am calling. We are looking for a regional representative for our products. You have an ideal background for this new position. In fact, we think you could help us define the job and its tasks. Are you interested in meeting next week to discuss the possibility?"

Amir was stunned. First, the social media thing worked, which he had not expected. Second, the job seemed like a great fit, not only aligning with his interests but one he could help shape. Third, getting a regular paycheck plus potential commissions was inviting after the ups and downs of store ownership. "Yes," he replied, "I'd be interested in discussing this possibility further." Although he had felt the sting of a setback, he climbed his way back to hope and created a new possibility.

As Amir realized, thumps to pride hurt. But recognizing them for what they are can help you prevent failure from being fatal. The people who care about you will empathize with your struggle, but they will be inspired by your perseverance. The people who only care about your performance may use your struggle to pat themselves on the back. Who cares? Jerks always take cheap opportunities to puff up their own pride.

As Teddy Roosevelt said, "It is not the critic who counts; not the man who points out how the strong man stumbles, or where the doer of deeds could have done them better. The credit belongs to the man who is actually in the arena, whose face is marred by dust and sweat and blood. . . ."[1]

Take the blow and recognize it for what it is. Go ahead and feel lousy for a moment, but then review, strategize, and try again. Find the fuel for improved performance, increased achievement, and deepened relationships. Hold onto the sustenance of uprising strength: hope.

Opportunity to Learn

We always face the temptation to give in after a setback, but you should regard failure for what it is: feedback. A quote frequently (but incorrectly) attributed to C. S. Lewis makes this point: "Failures, repeated failures, are finger posts on the road to achievement. One fails forward towards success." Failure is an invitation to learn. Cognitive scientists know that, suggesting that when we fail, we are in an optimal state to learn *if* we attend to our mistake. That willingness to be humble can fuel our efforts going forward, or pride and blame can stall our progress. It's a choice.

Dana was recently invited to serve as a conference keynote speaker. She prepared thoroughly and looked forward to the opportunity. While her presentation wasn't a complete failure—the content at least was good—her delivery fell flat. Did anyone take anything from the presentation? Maybe, but the response was more yawn than "Yippee!"

After a night's sleep and a yoga session the next morning, Dana reviewed her work while sitting in an airport. She immediately recognized that one section probably slowed the speech's momentum because it was out of place. She slowed down in midstream and lost the audience before her conclusion. Several weeks later, Dana offered a revised presentation, and the audience response was completely different. She "failed," examined her mistakes, and strategized a way forward. The failure was feedback that led to improvement.

You don't have to correct course alone. Sometimes you need to be open to advice from others. A mentor or instructor fits this role perfectly, as Brady discovered. After he completed a set, Brady placed the weights back in the J hooks, feeling dissatisfied. His trainer asked him what was up. "I'm not sure," Brady answered. "I know I have lifted more weight than that before, so I'm not sure why that felt difficult. It seems like I should be able to squat with that much weight easily. Maybe we should skip squats today."

"It could be several different factors making you feel that way" the trainer explained. "But I noticed your weight shift during most of those squats. Let's review form." Brady listened as his trainer reminded him of what his posture should be in order to center his weight. "Now, let's try the lifting motion with no weight on the bar."

Brady tried it again. His trainer kept reminding him of relevant details until Brady completed the motion several times correctly. "Now," said his trainer, "let's not skip squats. Let's do them right. Grab the same weights we had on there before, and add ten to each side."

A brush with failure is an opportunity to consider feedback that leads to improved performance. All of us occasionally let failure define us. We grouch at people for a few days. Maybe we attach blame elsewhere or offer excuses. When you frame the issue as feedback, though, even small setbacks can lead to improved performance. You get to choose the flexibility of humility, not the stiffness of pride, and do the work of converting failure into better approaches.

Lost or Bolstered

How we regard failure is not immune to outside influence. Let's say, on your own, you establish a baseline hope and a strategy to move forward. The people whose voices linger in your thoughts can deflate hope (and often decrease effort) or bolster hope (and increase effort.)

This is true of all of us. You might think you are immune to the influence of others, but you are deluding yourself. Even those who recharge best on our own are social beings. We all interact with others, and rubbing elbows leads to exchanged words, which then revolve in our thoughts. How many times have you found yourself mentally replaying a recent conversation? Our interactions with others contribute to our inner dialogues. As a result, people can tamp down or fortify your hope, and many people, often unknowingly, diminish hope.

It seems almost instinctual to temper people's hopes. Perhaps we're protecting them from over-hoping and underperforming. For some, their pride will take a hit if you are successful. Some people are just oriented toward the negative. Whatever the reason, others weaken rather than strengthen the hope of those looking for advice. The friend who hears you are taking up a new fitness routine and proceeds to tell you how they injured themselves doing a plank is, probably unintentionally, quashing your hope. The person sitting behind you in church who says, "I don't know why anybody would want to do that!" is, probably unknowingly, dampening your hope. The coach who suggests your recent setback is probably the best you can hope for is obviously dousing the flames.

Even those who love you and who think they are looking after your best interests may feel uncomfortable watching you struggle. Not recognizing their own unease, they try to protect you. Or, sometimes others may try to help but offer misleading suggestions or diagnoses.

My church congregation has loving people who consistently fortify my hope. If you asked anyone there about me, probably one of the first things they would tell you about is my running. Very few of them are runners themselves, yet they loyally track my fitness. They ask me about it and even listen as I discuss the ins and outs. They send me well wishes prior to and after races. They are all about helping me keep a strong and focused hope alive.

One morning, after I had eaten breakfast and gotten dressed for a race, my phone buzzed with a text message. I picked it up, expecting it to be a reminder from the race organizers. Instead, it was a message from a church member. "Hey. I just wanted you to know that I was thinking of you and cheering for you. Go get it!"

I should note that a community, such as a congregation, may aid your resiliency. In one study, female school superintendents consistently connected their resilience during very difficult circumstances to their religious beliefs.[2] Do you have a group that consistently has your back?

Some of us may find solace in merely a single friend. Ruby, for example, found groups of people more draining than energizing.

She relaxed best in solitude. With others, her shoulders tensed and she concentrated too much on interpreting others' communication. However, when she was discouraged, the solitude felt isolating, and Ruby sank into despair more often than she felt renewed.

The frustration and fatigue of the work week showed in Ruby's stumble into the lobby of her apartment building. Mrs. Evans from 6B looked up from her magazine and noticed a professionally dressed but profoundly discouraged neighbor.

"Sometimes the best you can say for a week is that it's over," Mrs. Evans called across the lobby.

Sighing, Ruby mumbled, "You're right. This is one of those weeks."

Striding across the lobby, Mrs. Evans smiled and said, "Come sit for a minute. Tell me about your drama-filled week."

At first, Ruby politely refused, but Mrs. Evans did not give up. The two settled into the lobby chairs, and an hour later, Ruby was laughing. More than that, she was uplifted and eager for the weekend. Friday chats with Mrs. Evans became part of Ruby's weekly schedule. Every Friday evening, Ruby placed a contented head on her pillow no matter how the work week had gone. She found someone who left her more hopeful. She found community.

Hope is attractive. Those who reinforce the hopes of others are magnets. We are drawn to them because they reinforce our potential and our best efforts. Hope thrives because they believe in us, even in those times when we lack such faith in ourselves.

Find these people. More important, be one of these people.

Permission to Hope

Maybe you are thinking: this sounds good, but only for other people. I've failed so many times, you may think, that I am afraid to hope again. Or, I have hoped so many times only to fail over and over again.

Or, my life is so full that I don't have time to do more than wish. All these feelings are valid. But they are also holding you back.

Remember, hope is risky. It offers no guarantees. How long have I been trying to run fast enough to qualify for the Boston Marathon? Years. Multiple attempts have come up short. A couple were close, but running isn't horseshoes. Close is not enough. Will I ever qualify for Boston? Some probably think I won't. I keep trying and failing. I hope and fail over and over.

My life is full. I'd have more time for things like writing if I just gave up on that hope. I understand what it is like to fear hoping again. And yet, right now, I am in the middle of a training cycle for yet another attempt.

You also have permission to hope again. Find a future that is challenging but possible. Develop a plan to move yourself toward that future that does not exist *yet*. Delight in things that go well along the way, and remember that setbacks and discouragement are temporary. Use setbacks as feedback. Learn what you can from them and apply that to your efforts going forward. Find your people—those who will bolster your hope so that when you lack wind in your sails, you have people who will re-inspire your hope. Hold on to that the outlook that makes achieving goals, strengthening social harmony, and climbing to new heights possible.

Don't let your past limit your future. There is a song lyric I especially like: "Whatever reminds you, don't let it define you."[3] You are capable of more. Hope is calling you to pursue something. Find it and work to make it happen. The same amount of time will pass whether you work toward goals or kick back and lounge your years away. The difference is what waits at the end of that time. Will you look back and think, "I tried, and I learned, and I am better as a result," or will regret add an unwanted weight to your memories? Neither of those futures exist yet. Choose hope.

CHAPTER 3

MINDSET

Failure can be a painful experience. But it doesn't define you.
It's a problem to be faced, dealt with, and learned from.
— Carol Dweck

Being on live TV, microphone in hand, thrilled Janice. Find the story, locate a knowledgeable storyteller, broadcast the news to the world—every part of the process energized her. At least at the start. Then Janice's sights become fixed on the anchor's chair. When an opening at the evening news anchor desk was announced, Janice submitted her resume and reached the final three candidates. She didn't get the job, but was offered an anchor position on the morning news.

Janice considered the morning news to be "fluff." The anchors might interview the city mayor, but then ask questions of a crack-of-dawn tai chi practitioner, a local quilting bee club, or other "soft news." "No, thanks," she told the station manager. She considered herself a serious journalist, and her pride would not squeeze into the morning anchor job. Eighteen months later, a colleague who had taken advantage of Janice's decision, was promoted from morning show host to the station's evening news anchor.

Luke had his sights fixed on a different sort of success. He loved Shannon and told her so, and she said she felt the same about him. In his mind, though, he wanted to hold off on marriage until his career could help sustain a comfortable life together. Such a desirable state was only one more promotion away. Luke would not settle for anything less than being a professionally "successful" couple. He never wanted to hear the phrase "struggling newlyweds." Time passed, and so did Shannon's patience. Luke's constant delay suggested a lack of sincerity in his feelings. As his success in business progressed, the relationship deteriorated. When "the" promotion came, Shannon was long gone.

We marvel at such stories. How could someone with that much promise make those decisions? Yet pride hijacks every member of the human race and puts us in places we do not want to be. In contrast, a "learning mindset" enables you to improve through strategic effort, and make wiser choices. Such a mindset believes an individual can accomplish merit by working. It refutes the idea that a person is as smart or as good or as accomplished as he/she can ever be.

Remember: mindset matters. The body cannot outperform the mind. Achievement cannot outpace the mind. Relationships cannot outgrow the mind.

Smart but Failing

When consulting in schools, I frequently encounter a "smart" student who is not performing up to their potential. Exasperated, the teacher explains that the student is not trying despite obvious intelligence. What's going on?

One possibility is that the student has a "fixed" mindset toward whatever tasks or subject matter he is being asked to master. His mental conversation goes something like this: "I made a mistake the first time I tried this, so I am obviously not good at it. It's safer to not try than to risk failing again."

Conceit cancels out his willingness to try. The student doesn't sense this connection. In his mind, he is practicing self-preservation. And frequently the student has the unintentional support of a parent. While expressing frustration about an assignment one evening, the well-meaning parent may have said, "You are probably not good at spelling because I was never good at it either." With just a few words, the fixed mindset is given a rational basis, and the student has a good reason not to try. Not trying is a guaranteed way of not succeeding. However, trying in even less-than-ideal conditions can sustain progress.

Take Randy, who had to buy new clothes. His recent weight loss made everything he had in his closet feel like he was wearing a larger person's clothes. He was. Those clothes belonged to a man who was 70 pounds heavier. A weekend shopping trip yielded clothes that fit. His coworkers complimented him on his new style. Regular walking, a healthier diet, and twice-a-week weight-lifting sessions changed more than Randy's body. His outlook was more positive, and he exuded happiness.

Then a tree root upended all his progress. Tripping over it sent Randy sprawling onto the wooded trail he'd been hiking. He twisted his ankle, badly. The doctor told him to stay off his feet as much as possible for six weeks. Although he was initially discouraged, Randy reviewed what had gotten him to this point—not focusing on the injury but on the transformation.

At that point Randy knew very little about diet and exercise. His first visits to the gym were more about learning than sweating. The weights, the machines, the posture and movements were all new to him. Randy thought, "Okay, so what I need to do now is get back into learning mode. I can't walk, but what *can* I do to maintain as much fitness as possible?" He made a phone call to a friend who had shown him the ropes in the gym. After explaining the situation, he asked for suggestions. The friend said, "I'll be right over. Open your garage door."

Soon his friend was setting up a few barbells, mats, and a weight bench in the garage. He explained that Randy could still focus on upper-body exercises without further injuring the ankle. He and Randy worked together on a plan. "This is not the end," his friend emphasized. "It just means you have to work differently while the ankle heals." Randy nodded, excited by the new challenges. Humility—that willingness to learn—kept Randy on track even though he was knocked off his feet.

Pride does just the opposite. It pushes us toward giving up, toward surrender right when we need to learn new ways to move forward. We often hear that pride comes before a fall. But sometimes a fall—or a setback—can reveal a new path waiting for us.

Religious texts overflow with both warnings about pride and praises for humility. The Torah, for example, points out that Moses, one of the greatest of men, was also the most humble. A Hasidic folktale illustrates how pride can even upend a "humble" individual. In it, a gentleman boasts to a religious scholar that he followed the rabbis' teaching and always avoided fame. The tzadik, knowing the man's heart, replies, "The trouble is that while you do run away from fame, you are always looking over your shoulder to see if fame is chasing after you."

Similarly, the Bible addresses the topic. Pride brings disgrace, but humility brings wisdom, claims a passage in the Old Testament. A story told in the New Testament focuses on a farmer whose pride demanded bigger barns. He tore down perfectly good buildings and built larger ones in their place. His untimely death the following night meant that he'd never reap the benefits of his bigger barns. The moral of the tale suggests that filling your barn with self invites such calamity. If we are not mindful of its negative influence, pride can steer our mindsets toward poor choices.

The Power of Pride

Pride masquerades as many things, preventing us from recognizing its impact on our lives. Self-preservation is just one of its disguises. It also masks itself as rationalization and blame—other forms of personal safeguarding. I didn't ace that test because the professor asked questions that were not included in the class notes. Or, I didn't get that job because the interviewer asked me unrelated questions. Sure, such explanations are partially true, but when they prevent us from upping our game, pride has done its destructive work. If you missed questions on the exam, how will you change your approach to studying for the next one? If the answers weren't in your notes, what will you do to make sure they are more complete next time? If some of the interview questions caught you by surprise, how will you strategically prepare for the next one? What topics can you learn more about to change the outcome of the next interview?

As C. S. Lewis stated, "The only people who achieve much are those who want knowledge so badly that they seek it while the conditions are still unfavorable. Favorable conditions never come." Blaming the conditions will just hold you back. They do matter, but shoveling all the blame there stifles your potential growth.

The coldest race I ever ran was in Charleston, SC. I woke up that morning, looked out the hotel window, and noticed the American flag over The Citadel was flying perpendicular to its flagpole. There was no ripple in that flag because the wind was constant. I groaned, already feeling defeated.

The race started out great. I was keeping a decent pace and was tucked into a group of runners keeping the same speed. Then we turned a corner. As we pushed up Charleston's main thoroughfare, the wind pushed back. It was cold, constant, and cruel. Okay, I thought, just get through this section. Since I was unfamiliar with the course, I didn't know that section would last for several miles—about half the distance of the race. By the time I reached the next turn on the course, I was miserable.

Guess what I did the rest of the day? Yep, I blamed the conditions. I didn't run well because of the wind. I mentioned that every time I told someone willing to listen. Did the wind matter? Of course. Was it the only reason, or even the main reason, that I didn't run a stronger race? No, but I allowed the wind to get in my head. I started blaming the conditions before the race even began. I didn't have a decent finish time because I justified not giving more effort. The body cannot out-perform the prideful mind.

Sometimes the circumstances are more complicated. Aaron did not mind the cold as he scooped ice cream every summer during high school. The job gave him an opportunity to interact with all kinds of people, provided some savings for college, and even a few bucks for fun. Returning home after his freshman year at State, he expected not only to be rehired, but to be brought back for the season as a manager.

The store owner greeted Aaron enthusiastically and proclaimed that one of the best scoopers in the business was back. Aaron beamed. "Are you back for the summer? Are you looking for a job?" the owner asked. Aaron said that he was and that he was hoping to be made a manager for the months he was here. "Hmm," replied the owner. "I have all the managers I need right now, but I really want you here. Customers love you!" As the owner paused to think of possible alternatives, Aaron's frustration grew. He had been a reliable worker for four summers. Didn't he deserve to be a seasonal manager this time?

"How about something new? What if you were a customer experience specialist? You would still be part of the scooping team, but your main focus would be making sure people have a good time even as they are making their flavor choices. I'll pay you nearly the same as a manager, but you won't have any of the responsibilities, and you'll still get a portion of the tips."

Aaron took a deep breath. His first thought was: what would he tell people he did for the summer? Explaining that he scooped ice cream would sound lame compared to his friends at State, who were working in their parents' businesses or in office buildings. Being a manager at least gave him some cred. "No, thanks," he replied. "I need to be a manager."

A few days later he found an office job in data management. It paid less, and he had to work different shifts every two weeks. He hated it, but he kept his pride, right? He was miserable about lower wages, but he could boast that he didn't buckle when offered less than a seasonal manager job. Is that winning?

Even when we fail, regroup, and try again, each subsequent defeat can make continued effort feel futile. At these times it is wise to reconsider goals and redefine what we will accept as success. But too frequently, we choose to quit rather than adjust. If I can't accomplish what I wanted to, we think, I'd rather quit than settle. We rationalize giving up by telling ourselves and others that we are determined not to compromise. Accomplishment cannot outpace the prideful mind.

For Alison it wasn't work that sparked a negative pride. It was a vacation day. As she paced, Alison deepened an obvious track in her living room carpet. That one day off—that was why it happened. Her best friend at work filled in willingly for her but failed to finish the project on time. Now Alison's boss was frustrated and made sure Alison was aware of it. Irritated, Alison lost her temper and said things she now regretted. Her best friend had turned away, returned to her desk, and not even looked at Alison the rest of the day.

"Did I say anything that was untrue?" Alison asked herself. "No," she thought. "Everything I said was true, so it's her problem if she is upset." In the back of her mind, Alison thought she might have been wrong for losing her temper, but she committed to the idea that she was completely right in her reaction. The rest of the week was tense, but Alison's pride prevented any attempt at reconciliation. Words between the two became merely functional. The relationship never returned to the joy the former friends had known.

Alison felt bad about the broken relationship, but proud that she had stood up for herself. So proud that learning from her poor choice wasn't possible. Friendship became friction, and ego kept the atmosphere charged with tension. Relationships wither before the prideful mind.

The Team of Grace and Strategy

Pride and the fixed mindset are powerful accomplices. One holds back our efforts while the other invents an alibi for not trying harder.

In contrast, the "learning mindset" is patient, strategic, and curious.

Patience provides the grace to grow. Curiosity examines failure and seeks places where changes could be made, and strategy provides the changes to make before or during the next attempt. A learning mindset provides: Grace for error, strategy for improvement.

We've all heard stories about natural talent, and these tales of easy routes to victory skew our thinking about achievement. This athlete was a natural at an early age and dominated the sport throughout her teenage years. This musician sat on a piano bench at the age of three and played the *Moonlight Sonata* from memory. His natural ability impressed judges at every competition, and now he solos with symphony orchestras. This trader loved numbers as a child and balanced her father's checkbook before she began kindergarten. Her natural ability has made her a huge success on Wall Street.

Yeah, we've all heard those stories. Here's a secret: they are not true.

Behind every natural talent lies a wealth of experience and hard work, as well as access to great role models, teachers, and coaches. (There's a reason Daniel LaRusso needed Mr. Miyagi.) Sustained interest also helps, as well as the individual's approach to developing their skills.

The first time we try anything, from multiplying fractions in math class to a bicycle kick on the soccer field to leading a group discussion, we rarely succeed. And if through some stroke of luck we do, we can rarely replicate the results on a second attempt. The reason? Initial skill learning is slow and deliberate. We practice one step at a time to achieve the desired result. Mastery, where we can perform a skill without thinking, takes time to develop. First, we establish accuracy, then we build efficiency.

That's why patience is a critical component of the learning mindset. First attempts require feedback and adjustment before additional tries increase accuracy. Space to learn, grace to accept mistakes.

This is true especially when trying something new. When Marshall first bought a bike, the technician explained how to pump up the tires. "All you need to do," he said, "is loosen this nut that allows air flow into and out of the bike tire." Marshall laughed at the simplicity of the solution.

His plans for the next morning hit a speed bump when he discovered his bicycle tires were soft. He grabbed the pump he had bought with the bike, attached the gizmo, and pumped. Air was going some-where, but not into the tire. He adjusted the valve head and tried again. No luck. Frustrated, he abandoned the bike and completed a different workout.

As Marshall calmed down, he reminded himself that cycling was a new pursuit. He wouldn't know everything immediately. Grabbing the pump once again, he headed back to the bike shop. After explain-ing the problem, the technician smiled and said, "Listen, many people have the same problem the first time they try using this pump. In fact, we need to do a better job of explaining how to use these before put-ting them in customers' hands." He re-explained that Marshall needed to loosen the nut first, and then attach the pump.

At first Marshall was frustrated. His plans for exercise had been blocked by a seemingly simple task. Then he found the patience he needed. He was just starting out, and it was okay to ask for help. His pride was not going to block his riding. Go get the answers you need, he told himself. All he needed was space to learn, grace to accept that he didn't know *yet*, and a humble willingness to admit that he couldn't succeed without help.

Think about a time you learned something significant. Perhaps you recall learning to play a major scale with two hands on a piano. It is unlikely that you found immediate success. You were probably slow and methodic, thinking your way through each step of the process. And you probably missed keys on that first try. If your teacher had allowed you to stomp off in frustration, you might never have tried a scale again. Most likely, the adult in your life encouraged you to give it another try. Better yet, perhaps she helped you examine the mistake you made and offered you a suggestion for how to avoid it on the next try. Both the encouragement and the feedback provided you with space to learn.

Feedback helps us be strategic. Think of the last time you faced a computer glitch. If you try the exact same approach that led to the error message the first time, your second attempt will not be any more successful. Something has to change. The learning mindset lets go of pride and pauses after a failed attempt to examine the error. Why? Feedback. Examining the error reveals how something could be done differently. Strategizing before the next attempt improves results. Mistakes are invitations to learn if, and only if, we are willing to attend to them and strategize before our next attempts.

Isabel used this approach following an unsuccessful audition. Her voice teacher filmed the audition, so Isabel had "tape" to review. When called, she walked onto the stage. The video showed that she looked down while getting into position instead of establishing early eye contact with the panel of decision makers. When asked what song she would be preforming, Isabel noticed that she answered softly, showing her lack of confidence.

The song itself went well. Isabel's voice soared in all the right places, and her interpretation was moving. The performance, Isabel realized, was exactly what she wanted it to be. Everything leading up to it, however, conveyed the wrong message for a leading role audition.

At her next voice lesson, Isabel shared her observations. Yes, her teacher confirmed, that was what she noticed too. For most of the lesson, they practiced entering and speaking confidently. Isabel found that she could do it when she was intentional about it. She had to purposely tell herself to stand up straight, make eye contact, and speak with a confident tone. As she stood backstage at the next audition, she mentally reviewed her plan. With her head up, smiling at the judges, she approached the center of the stage ready to take control. Grace for failure, strategy for improvement.

Imagine taking this approach to an interview when you didn't land the job. You may not have film to review, but you do have a memory of the meeting. How did you enter and introduce yourself? What did your body language suggest about your confidence and honesty? What questions forced you to make up answers that, on reflection, could have been better? Find the spots where feedback—from others or from your own analysis—suggests different strategies for the next interview.

Think of an activity you tried recently that did not go as well as you would have liked. Perhaps you tried cooking a new dish. Or had a rough parent-teacher conference. Or led an online conference call that did not accomplish much.

Replay the experience. Where did you make mistakes? What could you have done better? Now examine everything leading up to the failure. Could your preparation have been mapped out more strategically? If someone knowledgeable is available, ask him for feedback. If not, ask yourself how you might change your approach to be more successful the next time. Grace for error, strategy for improvement.

Elite athletes have a practice that illustrates this. Following a game or match or race, even if they won, they will review film of the event. They don't watch it to relive the glory, but to look for areas where a different strategy could be useful. Perhaps they notice an imbalance in their running gait, or an angle that is slightly off in their backhand, or a better location on the court to prevent an opposing player's shots. They look for anything they can improve before the next competition. This practice helped both teams make it to the 2018 Super Bowl.

The game pitted the Philadelphia Eagles against New England Patriots. These teams found themselves in one of football's most exciting championship games. A late-game comeback, a critical quarterback sack, both offense and defense playing at the top of their abilities—the game was exactly what fans hope a Super Bowl will be. Obviously the players at this level are skilled and physically shaped for the game, but that's true of the teams who didn't make it to the Super Bowl too. What contributes to one team winning a championship while others fall short?

Although the Patriots' Tom Brady and coach Bill Bellichick were known for their practice of reviewing video footage, the 2017-18 Eagles were equally committed to the practice. "I probably watch two hours a day on my own in addition to the meetings. We probably have three hours of meetings every day," Eagles safety Malcolm Jennings explained. Quarterback Nick Foles couldn't even come up with a number for the hours spent watching film each week. "There's a lot of it, of course. Every morning, we meet early and go to our quarterbacks room and that's what we do. We watch film. We look for things. And then we have meetings when we aren't practicing and we watch more. It's a lot, I know that. It takes up so much of the day."[1] Hours invested resulted in the Eagles' Super Bowl victory.

For these athletes, watching film is not a passive activity. They watch to process what they see in themselves, in opposing players, in team dynamics—any details that better prepare them for the next on-field battle. Failure is not the only experience that ignites the learning mindset; success should also spark review and strategizing. Professional athletes observe, and think seriously about what they see, all for the purpose of learning and growth. They maintain a curiosity about how to improve their play.

Curiosity Is Key

Curiosity is critical for sustained improvement. Even when we succeed, we can try for a better performance the next time. Curiosity leads to seeking improvements, ways to be stronger, ways to be better. This is especially true if your interest is a lifelong pursuit. You don't want to run one marathon, you want to race for several years. You don't just want to play "Chopsticks," you want to play works by classical masters. You don't just want to take one decent photo, you want to develop a growing portfolio of captivating images. *Curiosity is the force that sustains interest and improvement.* Without it, you are dependent on external motivation and recognition. Moments of glory are just that: moments. They cannot provide the consistent motivation needed to grow.

How can you know if you are curious? Asking questions is a sign. The brain does not like unanswered questions. It will keep pursuing answers even when you are not conscious—hence, the 2:30 AM solution to a problem you've recently encountered. If you find questions percolating in your head, continued effort in your chosen arena will remain rewarding.

The end goal need not be an achievement. Curiosity can help us in all walks of life. When Catherine's job required her to move from one region of the country to another, she found making new friends an unexpected challenge. She maintained contact with her friends in her old city, but longed for some company on morning walks, dinners, and weekend adventures.

While stirring her coffee one morning, she noticed the bulletin board at a cafe. She began to read the various notices. The local theater had an upcoming performance of an Agatha Christie mystery. A nearby church was holding a weekend fair to raise funds for an upcoming missions trip. A monthly dinner club was hosting its monthly meeting at a popular barbecue restaurant.

"Hmm," thought Catherine. "A dinner club. I wonder if I would meet some potential friends that way." She took a photo of the poster so she would have all the information. When she got home, she sent an email to the contact that was listed. What was the age range of the group's members? How did the dinners work—were there topics for them to discuss or was the conversation free flowing? How often did new members join the group? She tried limiting her inquiries, but her curiosity sparked a torrent of questions. She finished and pressed "Send" before she could talk herself out of it.

She received a reply later that afternoon. After reading the answers, she decided that she would go to the upcoming event. It seemed like a group she would enjoy. Thanks to following up on her curiosity, making new friends became a real possibility.

You may think of not think of moving as a setback. But when it comes to a person's social circles, it often is. Curiosity, that desire to know, can help one discover more than the sights to see in a new locale. It can lead you to people who will enrich your experience as long as you are there.

Sometimes finding such people can help you in a pursuit of new learning. For instance, Derek loved languages. Words had fascinated him since he could manipulate the magnetic letters on his mother's refrigerator. When he heard that "German has a word for everything," he decided it was a language he wanted learn. But how? His high school did not offer it. He googled different apps and online programs, but were any of them effective? How would he be able to practice pronunciation and conversation? So many obstacles—or as Derek saw them, questions.

He read reviews of various programs and studied the results from their research. He discovered a monthly German conversation group that met in the next town. He even found some beginning reader books in German. Soon he had assembled a collection of tools that could have him saying "*Guten Morgen. Wie geht es Ihnen?*" in no time.

This mindset—questioning combined with a determination to improve—is not always innate. Being upset over a poor performance is perfectly understandable, especially when preparing for the effort was a long process. I have crossed several finish lines feeling like I failed. I kept the pace for several miles but then lost it and finished slower than hoped. Was I disappointed? Every single time. And my wife can confirm that I am cantankerous for a while afterward. Thoughts of giving up float into consciousness, and my comments to her suggest that I feel stupid for even trying.

Fine. Let the poor result disappoint you, just don't be debilitated by it. If after 48 hours of frustration you are still beating yourself up, you will face the specter of quitting. Unless giving up is your goal, you have to find another way forward.

Moving beyond disappointment requires you to take back control of your internal monologue. Grace for error, strategy for improvement.

Blind Spots

Even if you have a learning mindset in one area, it does not guarantee that mindset in another. During a school visit, I had a few minutes between appointments, so I found a seat in the teachers lounge. Two teachers came in after me—let's call them Mr. English and Ms. Math. Their conversation went something like this:

> **Mr. English:** I do not know what I am going to do with Joanna. I can't get her to give any effort in my class. She doesn't complete homework, she refuses to write, and she seldom reads the literature assignments.
>
> **Ms. Math:** Are you talking about Joanna Student?
>
> **Mr. English:** Yes!
>
> **Ms. Math:** I can't believe that! Joanna is one of my best learners. She always has her assignments completed. She is one of the few who will ask questions in my class, and she's earning

top marks consistently. It's hard to believe we are talking about the same Joanna.

Mr. English: Yes, it really is. Hmm, wonder what is going on with her.

There could be many reasons for such an overt contrast, but mindset is a strong candidate. Joanna may have a learning mindset in math class ("I can get smarter through effort in this class"), and a fixed mindset in English ("I can't learn this kind of material. It's safer to do nothing than it is to try and fail."). She is open to trying, failing, and strategizing in math class—you can see her applying grace for error and strategy for improvement—but Joanna is set in her thinking about English class. Pride prevents her from even trying.

Why? Could be a million small influences that built up over time. Essays given back to her with so much red ink they looked like TV crime scenes. Comments made by previous teachers ("I'm sorry, Joanna, but you failed another English test"), suggestions from parents ("Don't worry, Joanna, I was never good at English either"), grading without strategic feedback ("Here is your paper, Joanna. You only earned a D on this one. You need to try harder"). Over and over, Joanna has been told that she's not good enough when it comes to English. Multiple dings to pride carve craters that create a false choice: quit trying or be a failure.

Surely, adults don't have these blind spots, right? Wrong. We do. Stop and identify one area where you automatically assume, "I could never learn to do that" or "I could never be good at that."

One reason is that we carry those thought patterns forward after schooling. For example, Ian did well with math until he reached high school. For whatever reason, though, he never connected with concepts in algebra and geometry enough to understand them. As a result, he began to tell himself that he was not good at math. Now, hold it a second, you might think. Doesn't he mean that he is not good in algebra.? Nope. Once we start letting pride dictate the messages we tell ourselves, it becomes natural to generalize.

That's why Ian breaks out in a sweat when his wife tells him he has to write a check to pay for the stove repairs. He can fill in the check with no problem, but then he has to subtract the amount from the checkbook ledger. "Wait! I'm not good at math!" he thinks. You're right: it is ridiculous, but it's true. Ian has a fixed mindset when it comes to his ability in math.

When he reached the required statistics class in his graduate studies, Ian's heart rate increased each time he sat at the computer. He *couldn't* understand the concepts. He *couldn't* learn the computer program. He *couldn't couldn't couldn't*. At least that's what Ian thought. The strategies the professor supplied appeared to work for his classmates. For Ian, the class sessions might as well have been spoken in Swahili. He was sinking, fast. Adding to his anxiety, the class was a week-long "intensive," and the students were expected to make presentations on the last day.

In desperation, Ian went to a local bookstore and purchased two books that suggested that even a dummy could learn statistics. He spent his evenings poring over the relevant chapters in both books. Slowly, some concepts began to make sense, but not until he drew illustrations of them. By Friday, Ian had a presentation ready. He identified the most important concepts that had been discussed during the week, sketched illustrations for each one, and then projected the images during his discussion.

He thought it was a rudimentary presentation, but several of Ian's classmates started saying, "Oh, now I get it!" His professor loved it, and Ian earned an A for his illustrated lecture. He went on to earn an A in the class, but not without much more work after the class sessions ended.

It turned out that Ian could be successful with math. He merely needed to buckle down and find his own way of processing concepts and related formulas. The fixed mindset is difficult, but not impossible, to overcome. We *can* shift our thinking to states that encourage continued effort.

Reclaiming Your Mindset

Having the humility and the curiosity to examine what went wrong or what could be improved nudges us toward resilience. Pride, concerns about what others think, the negative ways we view ourselves—these are the blinders that prevent us from looking back and examining our recent efforts. If we allow these blinders to remain, we ignore the very information we need to be more successful. Remember, when we make mistakes, we are cognitively in a prime place to learn from them.

The effort requires an objectivity that can be hard to find and maintain. You just experienced failure. You swam slower than you wanted to. Your new structure for making each morning more efficient caused more problems than it solved. You ordered dessert. You discovered the answer you gave on that algebra problem was wrong. What will you do?

Dr. Robert Brooks[2] offers a gateway to objectivity. He suggests phrasing your response to another's failure as follows: "This strategy you're using doesn't seem to be working. Let's figure out why and how we can change the strategy so that you are successful."

Beautiful! This conveys (1) that it's the strategy, not the person, that needs "fixing"; (2) that the individual is not being left on his or her own to process the error ("*Let's* figure out..."); and (3) that you believe in the individual's ability to ultimately be successful. This strategy can be helpful for self-reflection too.

Often failure exists on the everyday level. For instance, Stephanie was on a diet when the cake arrived for her daughter's birthday. Stephanie had been mindful of her diet through the entire afternoon. Then she carried the cake to the table. "A small piece," she thought. "I'll just have a bite." And she did. And then her daughter didn't finish her own piece. "I don't want it to go to waste," Stephanie thought. A few more bites. Then her own mother brought her a full piece, saying that Stephanie should at least celebrate on her own daughter's birthday. By the time the party ended, Stephanie had consumed far more calories than she intended. Later, she felt miserable about the lapse.

After a night's sleep, she could look back with a different perspective. "Okay," she thought, "I let the circumstances defeat me. Why?" She realized that she didn't have a plan for the rather predictable scenario. "Hmm, how could I have handled things differently?" She realized that her daughter's unfinished piece of cake could have been stored in the refrigerator for her daughter to eat later. When her mom showed up with that piece of cake, she could have thanked her, taken a bite, and then stored the rest of the piece for another family member to eat later. "That," she thought, "is how I will handle the next similar event." Then she reminded herself of her goal, why she was pursuing it, and got back to being intentional about her eating. Grace for error, strategy for improvement, failure as feedback.

Now, how can you apply this to your own thinking? Perhaps use an outline like this: "Okay, the way I just tried to achieve my goal was not successful. Let me see if I can figure out why and how I can change my approach so that I am more likely to succeed." Such self-talk can help you (1) focus on the strategies rather than your feelings about failure; (2) direct your attention to what you can control or change going forward; and (3) reaffirm your belief in your ability to reach your potential. It can reorient your mind for physical performance, social success, and goal achievement. Changing how we perceive and label challenges can help too.

Reframe

A few years ago, my wife and I encountered a pair of brothers with a unique skill. They own a fine art and framing shop, and shopping in their store is always entertaining. I can pick any piece of art, hand it to one of them and say, "Frame this." They will place at least three different frames on the painting that completely change the way I see it. Sometimes the frame affects the colors. Sometimes the frame affects the depth. Sometimes the frame affects how my eye travels through a painting. It is a remarkable phenomenon that you have to experience to fully appreciate. With nonstop commentary and humor, these brothers can transform your experience with a painting.

Reframing is helpful when pursuing goals and facing hardships. Instead of seeing obstacles as insurmountable stressors, a shift in perspective—a new frame—views them as challenges or opportunities for growth. This positive thinking does not deny reality; it is not looking on the bright side. (By the way, research indicates that telling someone to "look on the bright side" actually makes the person feel worse.) It's the direct opposite. It recognizes reality, but rather than groaning and giving up, it enables you to strategize ways to surmount the challenges.

Can reframing your thinking make a difference? Yes. Not only will it influence the effort you give in pursuit of your goals, it may also keep your brain tissues healthy. Recent studies have found a correlation between frequent negative thinking (giving up, blaming the circumstances) and earlier onsets of dementia.[3] So, if you can't find a good reason for a different perspective, consider working for it to protect yourself.

One reason I like running is its mental aspect. Being in great shape helps, of course, but the endurance and stamina required calls upon different faculties. You can fight yourself, or you can decide to gut it out.

Running's next door neighbor is biking, and I've had friends relate very similar experiences to my own. One of them, Terry, entered a race in Tennessee. The morning of the race, Terry looked out the hotel window. At a glance he saw that it was very windy. Groan. (Yes, it's okay to groan as long as you don't let it rule your day.) The bike race would be cold and miserable.

Terry thought: Okay, it's likely going to be a factor in the race. It's an added challenge. So, to still chase my desired finish time, what should I do? When I'm not riding into the wind, I can increase my speed a bit—not an extreme amount because I need the energy to complete the distance, but a slight boost will help with my time. I am in good enough shape to do that. When I face the wind, which will definitely happen at some points, I will think of it like a hill, which means I will give extra effort. I won't fixate on my speed in these sections. Instead, I will maintain the same amount of energy I've been giving in the sections where the wind is not in my face. That should give me my best possible finish time. If I still miss my goal, it will be okay. I will know that I pushed through the challenge and gave my best performance.

By reframing the event, Terry found a way to cross the finish line in excellent time. He gave a sterling performance on a day that required overcoming adversity. The story told afterward was one of triumph, one that inspired others.

If you remember my earlier tale about facing the wind in my own race, you can see: Terry did everything right that I had done wrong.

I let my initial groaning control my effort. However, sometime after the race, I was able to examine the failure. I figured out why I had performed so poorly. I knew that I could change my strategy, and therefore, be successful. That's the power of the learning mindset. Missteps get broken down rather than beating us up. We strategize rather than shrink, and grow rather than groan.

Have you failed recently? Did a physical achievement elude you? Did a relationship suffer from a momentary lapse in civility? Did a long-term goal get interrupted? Find the humility necessary to examine the failure and make the setback a stepping-stone to smarter effort. *Don't let defeat define you.* With a learning mindset, setbacks can become launch pads for success. Cultivate the uprising mindset.

CHAPTER 4

GRIT

If you don't rule your mind, your mind will rule you.
— Eliud Kipchoge

andice and Audrey felt like their lungs were on fire. The final lap of the 400-meter freestyle had them both swimming at the edge of their endurance. Commentators described the race between them as being neck and neck. Candice's brain was screaming, "Quit!" Audrey's brain was screaming, "What are you doing?" Their thoughts pleaded with them to stop stroking.

The commentators noticed the moment it happened. Candice eased up, barely slowing her pace but enough that Audrey shot into the lead. In fact, Audrey increased her pace in the final strokes before touching the wall first. Candice had to settle for third as the swimmer in the lane next to her took advantage of her slower strokes and claimed second place.

What made the difference? Both swimmers were at the top of their games. Both were accustomed to winning races. Both understood what racing felt like in its final moments. But on this day Audrey dug deep and found grit while Candice surrendered to the desire for relief.

Grit, while sounding like something you might wash off your feet, gets a lot of positive press. We could all meet our New Year's resolutions if we just had more grit. Our children would be more successful in and out of school if they were more gritty. We're frequently reminded that grit correlates with achievement in an endless number of areas.

But what is grit? While a learning mindset helps us improve following failure or success, grit keeps us going during our attempts. Brad Stulberg[1] defines it as "experiencing something that is subjectively distressing, and then leaning in, paying attention, and creating space to take a thoughtful action…" That sounds like significant thinking is involved, like it might take time to construct right when you do not have time to give. However, if the right foundation is laid before an event, grit can be found quickly.

This may not fit with what you see in role models of grit. These people seem to possess a quality the rest of us lack, as if they were born with grit just like some were born with brown eyes. Since it appears this way, it's easy for the rest of us to let ourselves off the hook. We weren't born with what they've got, so it's understandable if we grind to a halt rather than find the grit to hustle.

Jada unfortunately believed this lie. For a year she loved meeting with local writers a few times each month. She enjoyed the interaction and valued the feedback. She strengthened several of her poems as a result of the group's input. Feeling good about her work, she submitted a poem to a national poetry magazine that another writer in the group mentioned. When the other member's poem got accepted and published but Jada's did not, she felt deflated.

At the next meeting, the other writers encouraged Jada to revise another of her poems. They loved the imagery and the tone and speculated that magazine editors might agree. Jada sighed. Her best effort was never good enough. The group always had feedback. The editors had not liked her last submission. She just did not have what other poets did. She pulled out the poem the next morning, and rather than working on it, she regarded it as evidence of her failure. Discouraged, she quit writing for several months. Others had it. She did not. So why try? She didn't find the grit needed to continue.

One problem with our discussion of grit results from how we use the word. We *grit* our teeth, for example. In fact, when you think about the concept, you may imagine someone with a clenched jaw pushing through a seemingly insurmountable task. He grits his teeth and forces himself to study the periodic table of elements. She grits her teeth and pushes her way through three more pushups. The child grits his teeth and, somehow, manages to eat the detested carrots.

Actual grit is not quite that dramatic because it is a decision. By the time teeth are clenched, grit is already present.

A Mindset

Grit is a mindset, which is good news for those of us desiring more of it. A *mindset*, according to the dictionary, is an attitude, disposition, or mood, an intention or inclination. We develop mindsets through experiences and our responses to them, but you can change your mindsets through conscious choice. As we saw in the last chapter, our mindset as we approach learning determines our willingness to put effort into mastering something new. But when the going gets tough, when learning or trying to achieve or an attempt to reconcile becomes challenging, we need another mindset: grit. Caroline Adams Miller[2] suggests developing grit is more than an option, stating, "… building authentic grit isn't just possible but…it's our duty to do so if we want to live in a world that upholds standards of excellence and shuns quitting." If you want to move ahead, you cannot ignore the mindset you adopt when circumstances test your resolve. You can choose to proactively prevail, or you can wallow in the wish that your circumstances will change.

Bad weather and David's tight schedule meant he had to complete a workout on a treadmill. He always struggles with staying on the machine long enough to complete the cycle. He's tried all the usual distractions (e.g., music, podcasts) with no luck. He watches the data readout on the treadmill constantly, which just reminds him how much farther he has to run. After 15 minutes of this, his mind was screaming for relief from the tedium. David's body was not fatigued, but his brain was. "Please," it begged, "hit the stop button, and then let's think about dinner."

Grit is what we need in such moments. Don't stop and dwell on the struggle. Don't quit and blame your circumstances. Create space and take intentional action.

David knew that he needed to find a way to persevere. Step one was figuring out a way to stop staring at the scrolling data readout. Since he had music playing, he made a rule: he could not look at the treadmill screen until the chorus of each song came along. That wasn't a lot of time between glances, but it was enough for him to feel like he was making progress, and making yourself aware of progress nourishes motivation. Second, David needed to find a way to distract his mind between those glances. He decided to alternate between repeating a mantra and counting his breathing cycles. That gave his brain something else to focus on other than the recurring foot strikes on a looping belt. At the end, he not only completed the workout, but he did it with a faster pace and even added some distance.

That does not mean that David is eagerly anticipating his next treadmill run. He will probably struggle with motivation and perseverance again. However, if he can accept and thoughtfully address the unpleasantness, grit will get him through.

Like David struggles on the treadmill, Mildred struggles with monotonous tasks. Working in a factory that produces highly specific components for weapons systems means occasionally making the same tiny part over and over. Once a month, Mildred has to produce short, thin metal rods. These have to be individually cut and precisely measured. It is a repetitive task but demands intense concentration. When a rod is even a hair too long or too short, the saw has to be recalibrated.

Mildred groaned when the latest day arrived on the calendar. How would she make it through without getting glassy eyes, losing her concentration, and increasing her injury risk? She knew that rushing was not the answer. That led to mismeasured parts and more frequent calibration of the saw. As she started, she wondered how many rods, on average, she cut before calibration was needed. She started keeping track. After a few dozen, Mildred cut a rod that was too long. She calibrated the saw and began counting again, trying to beat that number. This time she produced slightly more than three dozen rods before recalibration was needed. She kept track all morning, always trying to beat the previous number.

Her supervisor wandered by and asked her how it was going. "Great!" Mildred replied. She was as surprised as her supervisor by her response. A few minutes after that, she was finished. She handed off a tub of precise steel rods to the department where they would be added to a larger part. Returning to her work area, she noticed that she had completed the task about an hour faster than last month, and she felt good about her work.

Such "gamifying" of a task is one way to find grit. It reframes the task for the mind, making it something worth pursuing rather than drudgery to be endured. Got to practice those boring scales on the clarinet? See if you can reduce the number of mistakes each time (actually count), and then see how quickly you can play each one smoothly. Have to attend a dinner meeting you'd rather avoid? Choose an unusual word or two— *Brobdingnagian* and *ambrosial,* perhaps—and see if you can naturally weave them into conversation. Release your mind from thoughts of drudgery by finding a goal to pursue. Distraction can be grit's best teammate.

A Choice

Applying strategies such as gaming a task is one way to choose grit. While striving to accomplish something, you will make hundreds of decisions about when and how hard to push, and when and how much to ease up. The effect is cumulative, meaning that these moment-to-moment decisions influence the outcome.

Joel chose his way to push past writer's block, even though the route there presented its own challenges.

It started while Joel was on a work trip. His normal routine—an early morning bike ride followed by time to write before work—was upended by client meetings. Afterward, a short run and weight workout led to dinner, and by the time he was back in his hotel room, he was too mentally tired to put words together. He wasn't sure it mattered; he'd struggled with the chapter he was currently writing even when he was home.

The second morning during breakfast, he pulled out a pen. He jotted down his schedule, looking for any opening where he might squeeze in some writing. There wasn't any. On paper, it looked as impossible as it had seemed in reality. Giving up on writing for the full week was justifiable but not satisfying. Okay, he thought, how do I use the time I do control? When no easy solution was evident, he chose to keep looking.

He began listing the activities he did before and after his client meetings. Mornings were spent getting ready for the day, packing up supplies, ironing a shirt, eating breakfast on the hotel's schedule, and driving 20 minutes to the worksite. All that, he thought, is necessary. What about my evenings? When he returned to the hotel, tired from the day, he collapsed on the bed and watched a little TV before getting ready for bed. He knew trying to write at that time would be fruitless. Circumstances seemed insurmountable. Still, Joel looked for an answer.

Are there times I could control? he asked himself. He was used to getting up early. His usual bike rides started just before dawn. He got up at the same time he did at home, but the hotel didn't serve breakfast for another 90 minutes. He used most of that time preparing for the day, but what if he decided when breakfast was served? All that required was picking up breakfast items he could keep in his room. That by itself did not open up an obvious block of time. Joel sighed. Maybe there really was no time to find. He stared at his notes and chose to keep searching.

What about his evening? No, he couldn't write, but could he do anything to free up other time? Hmm, all that ironing and packing up he did in the morning while awaiting breakfast—that could be done in the evening. It didn't require much thinking. He could even watch TV while he did it. With that, suddenly about 45 minutes opened up each morning. Okay, he decided, this begins today. After dinner, he stopped to pick up breakfast items. When he got back to his room, he immediately began getting everything ready for the next morning. He decided to keep looking when no obvious time could be found. He chose his way to possibility.

The next morning, settled into a cafe near his worksite, Joel stared at his laptop. Finding the time had not overcome his writer's block. The chapter just didn't flow, and neither did the words to fix it. Joel closed his eyes and took a deep breath. There was something he recalled from a recent writers' conference. What was that activity the workshop leader led them through?

Recalling its main steps, Joel assumed the perspective of his main character. The central event of the chapter was a turbulent family reunion featuring a cookout at a state park. He wrote, "Let me tell you the truth about family reunions." Writing as his protagonist, Joel launched into a tirade that came as quickly as his fingers could type. Little of this text would make into the chapter, but the exercise helped him discover the angle from which the reunion would engage the reader and move his story forward.

Notice the multiple places where Joel had to choose his way forward. Each of those decisions is a gritty choice. At no point did Joel grit his teeth and "power through." (Although even "powering through" is a choice!) Such an approach would not have accomplished much. Joel had dual challenges: scheduling his writing and getting past writer's block. Neither of these obstacles could be surmounted without thoughtful decisions. When you confront conditions that challenge your stick-to-itiveness, be like Joel: choose your way to grit.

That's exactly what Marta had to do as she faced her closet. Years of shoving stuff in wherever it fit had created a briar-like tangle of chaos. Each item would need to be removed, evaluated, and either thrown out or kept. Then the desired items would have to be placed back in the closet in some sort of coherent order. The temptation to close the door and ignore it for another day pushed hard on Marta's resolve. No, she decided, today would be the day.

An hour later, only one of the closet's five shelves had been cleared. "One is good," Marta thought. "Maybe I could do one each weekend." While that was a workable plan, Marta knew it wasn't optimal.

To know what she had, what should be grouped together, and how to best utilize the space, she needed to continue.

"Okay," she thought. "How can I help myself push through this until it's completed?" That question moved her toward grit. *She chose to search for a solution rather than quitting.* Many times, committing to a task will arm you with the grit you need.

Deliberate Practice

Photography has come a long way since the daguerreotype. When I was growing up, you had to have physical film in a camera to capture a picture. And you had to shoot all the photos in the roll before seeing the results, so the last picture you took could be months later than the first one. Once the roll was filled, you took the film to a place and paid the people there to convert your film-trapped images into photographs you could see and handle. Frequently, you would be surprised to see what you had captured. The photos were taken so long ago that you forgot that you took them!

We use the term *develop* to describe the seemingly magical transformation from film to photograph. What was imprisoned on film did not stay as it was; it was developed into something better. It took a lot of time and effort to evolve from shot to show.

This idea is perfect for a discussion of grit. Grit, like old-time film, can be developed. You can be grittier than you are today. How do you do it? You practice.

That does not mean you sit around grinding your teeth and thinking, "I will get grit. I will get grit." What develops grit is the same type of practice you engage in to develop your skills. Researchers refer to this as "deliberate practice." It requires *intentionally working just beyond* your current expertise, abilities, or endurance. If you simply repeat what you've already accomplished, you are not engaging in deliberate practice. You have to push slightly beyond that. This develops your proficiency and your grit.

Let's examine this via childhood piano lessons. You have learned to play one octave of the C-major scale on the piano. You know the right hand fingering: 1-2-3-1-2-3-4-5. Your teacher explains that now you will add the left hand to the scale. The fingering is different. The crossover point, where the hand actually moves up the keyboard, is different. And putting this together with the right hand is beyond your current abilities. It's going to get frustrating before it gets perfected.

Slowly, over and over, you practice one octave with two hands. Your fingers get tangled. You might feel like you will never get it right. In this moment, you can surrender and stop trying, or you can find a reason to keep working.

Let's fast-forward a few years. You are swimming laps. Your training plan calls for you to swim 10 percent farther than you ever have before. At some point, this gets difficult. You know that you only need a few more laps, but you are feeling like you'd rather quit, hit the showers, and find a cafe where you can relax and recover. You can get out of the water and grab your towel, or you can find the grit to keep going.

To develop grit, *you have to reach these points*—the moments where you have a choice. And you have to practice choosing strategies that spark grit.

You may be tempted to argue that people with natural ability do not need grit because they never have to practice something that much. In their book *Peak: Secrets from the New Science of Expertise*, Anders Ericsson and Robert Pool[3] make a convincing case for there being no such thing as "natural ability." The examples that people use to argue for it fall apart when they are carefully investigated. One classic case is Mozart.

Mozart's father was a pioneer—someone who was ahead of his time in training young musicians. Specifically, Leopold Mozart engaged his son in frequent deliberate practice. When Mozart began public performances, he demonstrated what motivation and years of deliberate practice can produce.[4] Natural ability? Nope. Effective teaching? Yep. Mozart was probably a man of immense grit, at least when it came to music because he constantly practiced just beyond his current abilities.

To develop your own grit, you need to practice like Mozart. You need to frequently find yourself at a spot that requires choosing to continue rather than quit. When you face that choice, how do you find grit rather than giving up? You choose your way to uprising.

What Do You Value?

Values are the ideas by which you navigate your life. You can also rely on them when you need grit. For example, one of my core values is preparation. When I am invited to teach or speak, I spend days putting my notes together and developing the resources I want participants to have. When I go into a race, I use a packing list to make sure I have everything I need, and then I lay it all out the night before the race. I prepare thoroughly. When I need grit, one truth I can tell myself is that I am prepared for the challenge. I can find my way to grit by reassuring myself that I am, indeed, prepared.

Now let's look at a person who values creative thinking. Whenever a situation fails to evoke a positive emotion, Briana imagines what changes are possible. At her church, for instance, she found an area that appeared unwelcoming and it was just inside one of the main entrances. She stood back, surveyed the space, and imagined possibilities. A welcome booth with coffee? A seating area? A big sign saying, "Welcome!"? One thing was certain: the area would be getting a makeover soon. Briana wouldn't rest until the right vision became reality. Money would be found, the right objects would materialize, and the area would be welcoming. The challenges were no match for Briana's core value-powered grit.

How can you make values work for you? First, choose goals that have meaning beyond yourself. Want to pursue a promotion at work? Find a reason other than financial gain to put forth the effort. Want to win your age group in an athletic competition? Find a reason other than personal pride to pursue it. Want to get to know that new member of your book club? Find an intention other than wanting to mine his thoughts before stating your own.

Selfish goals frequently generate low standards. If you want the promotion at work merely for your own monetary gain, you will likely play the political games of your employer rather than actually developing the skills and giving the effort that would earn you the promotion. If you want to win your age group just so your name will be announced at the awards ceremony, your satisfaction with the accomplishment will be short-lived. If you want to make a new friend just to move ahead of others in a discussion, you will fail to invest in the friendship and your "friend" will feel used.

Now, what if the promotion at work was worth pursuing because it will encourage your own development and put you in a position where you could help others grow? You value growth, knowing that it is the gateway to fulfilled potential. You push yourself to be better and you equip others to be better because wasted potential runs counter to a core value.

What if the age group award was worth pursuing because it would inspire others your age to pursue excellence? You value inspiration because you know it is an intrinsic motivator. You allow yourself to be inspired, and you love inspiring others. You push yourself so that you model the way forward for others because accepting the status quo runs counter to a core value.

What if that new friendship was worth cultivating because you wanted to get and give reading recommendations beyond what you read for the book club? You value new experiences and the wisdom of others. You find suggestions from other passionate readers expand your horizons, and you have helped others discover new works and new authors. These shared reading experiences have created opportunities for engaging discussions and have deepened relationships.

Now, let's see how these core values can empower grit.

Let's take a rough day at the office. It started with spilled coffee, included a disagreement with a co-worker, and involved a tense conversation with a disgruntled client. The day seems like a complete waste. You could grump along until 5:00, biding your time until you can escape, or you can find the grit to press on despite the setbacks. You value growth. So, you reflect on what you could control in the two people-related issues. You identify new strategies for addressing the issues, and you seek out the co-worker to mend fences. You call back the client and offer a new proposal to satisfy their complaint. Through grit you dismissed your wounded ego, reflected on your core values, and achieved reconciliation.

And the age group award? At Mile 11 of a half-marathon, thoughts of giving up push into your mind. You need grit and you need it now. This moment, you realize, is where inspiring others is a real possibility. If the race were easy, how would it encourage others when they face inevitable challenges? This is not for a moment; this is for influence. You beat back the opposition of your mind and find a way to a strong finish. Grit accessed via your core value, the mind enabling physical performance.

Or, consider that potential new friend, When you suggest meeting at a local cafe to "talk books," you can't find any mutually available dates. You start to feel defeated and consider forgetting the idea. Then you realize that those new reading experiences and insight-rich conversations cannot happen without continuing to try. You suggest a different time and place. "What if we met for lunch on Sunday afternoon?" That works. You resisted giving up and veered in a different direction. You stuck it out, went the extra mile.

So, what are your values? If you don't know, how do you figure it out? In their excellent book *Peak Performance*, Brad Stulberg and Steve Magness[5] provide some guidance:

1. Identify five core values. For example, in identifying the values related to my coaching of runners, I choose: achievement, education, inspiration, pragmatism, and self-control.

2. Clarify/define each of the five. For example, here is how I expanded mine:
   achievement: to discover true limits by pushing to surpass current ones
   education: to learn and share learning with others
   inspiration: to motivate and equip others to pursue improvement/growth
   pragmatism: to search for solutions until what works is discovered
   self-control: to prove what commitment and perseverance can achieve

3. Rank your values from the most important or influential to the least. The top three probably capture the essence of your core values.

Stulberg and Magness recommend one final step, which builds on the identification of your core values. This final step results in a "purpose statement." For example: My purpose in coaching runners is to be the best coach I can be, through modeling and education, so that others are inspired and equipped to surpass limits and pursue growth.

What are the values related to your area of pursuit? Identifying them provides you with a gateway to arming yourself with grit the next time you encounter struggle. But what do you do with those core values when you need to work through a phase of discomfort?

The "Calm Conversation"

Steve Magness[6] coined the term *calm conversation* to name the internal interaction an individual should have when facing challenges. In other words, the type of self-talk that should be our go-to when we need to find grit. This "calm conversation" includes the following elements:

1. Acknowledge the discomfort you feel: "Okay, this is starting to hurt," or, "Hmm, I am angry and feel like I want to strike back."
2. See the discomfort as part of pursuing your purpose: "I am pushing hard *because* I have a goal to achieve," or, "I am impatient *because* I want to react but my response needs to be strategic."
3. Reframe: "This is just the feeling of effort, not injury, I am fine," or, "This feeling shows that I care about the process and the result, I just need to keep both positive, and I can do that."

The key is to connect the immediate felt experience to your values. This hurts *because* I am pursuing a worthy goal so I can inspire others, not: This hurts and I am just going to suffer until I quit. I am impatient *because* I am growing into someone who can spark growth in others, not: I am impatient so I will speak my mind and score a point. I am feeling defeated *because* I'm hoping for new and interesting conversations, not: I am feeling frustrated so this probably isn't going to work. Reconnecting with your values provides a reason to keep pushing or to try a different tactic or to pause and strategize. As Stulberg[7] suggests, focusing on fighting pain creates the experience of suffering, and suffering rarely leads to grit. Rather than allowing your thoughts to shape your perspective, direct your mental spotlight onto the thoughts themselves, and talk back to them: "Thanks for your opinion, but I'll handle this."

Researchers claim that positive self-talk influences our perceptions of effort. Negative self-talk makes what we're doing feel significantly harder. It quickens breathing rate and increases levels of cortisol—a stress hormone. You can talk yourself into failure, but you can also talk yourself into success. In one study, participants who received training in positive self-talk lasted nearly 20% longer on a cycling test than the control group. These test subjects rated the test as being easier than an attempt they completed before the self-talk training.[8] Your mental monologue really does matter.

The workout was tougher than Derrick expected. He made getting fit before he turned 50 a major goal. Now, six months away from his birthday, he was seriously questioning the sanity of such a pursuit. He had joined a gym, found a trainer, and showed up for his first session. At first the tension in his working muscles felt fantastic. Now, they felt more like rubber, and completing each set required willpower. This does not feel good, he thought, and it's going to feel worse tomorrow. Why am I doing this?

"Come on, Derrick! Two more reps. You've got this." Derrick forced himself to finish, but then slumped back onto the bench.

"I don't know if I can do this," he sighed. "I've never worked out like this, and maybe I am starting too late."

"Oh?" said the trainer. "You told me you wanted to be the fittest you've ever been in six months. Have you changed your mind?"

"No," replied Derrick. "That is still what I want, but I don't know if I can do this enough to get there."

"What are you focusing on right now?"

Derrick thought a moment. "On how much this hurts. On how much it's going to hurt tomorrow. On how much it will hurt every time."

"Ah," nodded the trainer. "So you're suffering, right? Or at least you think you're suffering."

"No, I really am suffering," laughed Derrick.

"Yeah, that's because you are only focusing on the discomfort and not on the fact that working out is part of your plan. That working out like this is how you get to your goal."

"I know that I need to work out," sighed Derrick.

"Why?" asked the trainer. "Why do you want to work out?"

"Well, I'm not going to be fit by not exercising."

"Okay," said the trainer, "so let's figure out how to change your head so your body can move ahead. Why are you suffering?"

"Because you're making me do this workout!" Derrick chuckled, trying to keep his exasperation from showing.

"No, see, that's the problem," explained the trainer. "You are focusing on the feeling without connecting it to your goal. Try again. Why are you uncomfortable?"

Derrick sighed. He didn't like these questions. They were forcing him to think beyond his immediate feelings. However, something started to connect. Why was he uncomfortable? Wait. Uncomfortable? That's not the same as suffering. He took in a breath to argue this point but then hesitated. "I am uncomfortable because I want to get fit. I want to achieve the goal I have for myself."

"So then, this current feeling is not suffering, right?" asked the trainer. "It's part of the feeling that results *because* you are working toward a goal."

"Yeah. Okay," said Derrick. "It's the feeling of progress, then?"

"That sounds like a good perspective," smiled the trainer.

"Okay," Derrick said. "What's the next exercise?"

Derrick's birthday party celebrated five decades of life and a newly-fit quinquagenarian. His trainer even joined in the festivity.

Acknowledge, connect to your values, and reframe. Talk yourself into sticking it out. That grit will allow you to scale new heights.

Mind Your Mantra

Repeating a mantra, or a short phrase that captures a beneficial thought, is a helpful tool. It prevents the brain from obsessing over your current discomfort and vividly painting worst-case scenarios on your mental canvas. It has a calming effect, elevating you from panic to a place where you can carry out a calm conversation. This happens, in part, because repeating a mantra quiets your prefrontal cortex, where your personal disaster movies are produced, and because it boosts dopamine levels in the brain.

What should your mantra be? It's a highly individual thing. One of mine is "Give the effort." It reminds me to push when training makes me feel like quitting. A mantra that I recently "borrowed" comes from mountaineer Jimmy Chin[9]: "Commit and figure it out." This reminds me to connect with my values and treat the current struggle as a problem to be solved rather than suffering to be endured.

How does this work in practice? Avery has the challenging job of telephone marketing. He frequently makes cold calls to potential clients, hoping to inform them of his employer's products and services. As you might imagine, people abruptly hang up on Avery on a frequent basis, and that's when people actually answer his calls. "It can be discouraging very quickly," he explains. "I wanted to quit after the first hour I was in the job. However, it's a good company with great opportunities for advancement." He knew that he would need a way to keep himself positive through long spells of rejection.

One day during a break, he was trying his best to psych himself up. "I thought, 'Okay, I am going to make one more call. I can do that.'" He did, and got no answer. "One more call," he told himself. Before he knew it, that phrase—*One more call*—became his personal rallying cry. "I know that if I can make one more call, and keep making one more call, eventually I will make a sale. I just had to find a way to talk myself into making the next call."

Avery deploys this mantra several times a day. When he finds he can't generate a positive attitude for that next call, he takes a break. "It's crazy," he says, "but that simple phrase keeps me moving forward until, before I know it, the work day is over. I can commit myself to another call because I like the idea of progress." He explains, "Each call that goes unanswered or that gets cut short puts me closer to the one where I'll be able to connect with a client. So, every call is progress." A mantra that works with a value Avery holds—a good combination for stoking grit.

If you were developing a slogan for your core values, what would it be? That's a good way to brainstorm possible mantras. Find a few, then try them out. The one that helps you find the grit to keep pursuing your goals is the keeper. Deploy that mantra to quiet your brain when you face moments where you need to travel beyond the exit ramp of surrender.

Look Ahead and Be Grateful

Rather than worst-case scenarios, put your prefrontal cortex to work for your benefit. Bi-directional thinking—looking back and/or looking ahead—can help you find grit.

Looking back means directing your mind to what enabled you in the past to pursue a worthy and meaningful goal. Specifically, to look back with gratitude. Who helped you along the way? Who has cheered you on? Who has given you great advice? Spend several moments expressing gratitude for these people. If needed, thank them out loud, whether they hear you or not. Simply expressing gratitude has been shown to foster grit.

Summoning such a memory can be challenging in practice. Let's consider Mandy, a barista when she had to deal with a difficult customer.

"The drink isn't right," he insisted. Mandy had made exactly what was entered into the computer, but the customer saw it differently. Graciously, she apologized and offered to remake the drink. "It should have been right to start with," contended the customer. "My order was very clear."

Mandy verbally reviewed his order and he confirmed that it was correct. Mandy then asked him what about it did not taste right. "I don't know. You made it. You should be able to figure it out," he argued. Mandy remade the drink and handed it to the customer. He tasted the drink, proclaimed that it still wasn't right, and huffed out of the cafe, carrying the drink he claimed was substandard.

Mandy could feel her blood pressure rising. She took a breath, closed her eyes, and asked herself what she was doing there. She thought back to the early morning, when her manager had begun training Mandy for a management position. She thought about the friends she had in the other baristas. She remembered the regular customers who were always a bright spot in her days. Soon, she found herself mentally thanking each individual who helped her get where she was. Her next customer was greeted with a grateful smile while Mandy pushed through the work day with a renewed spirit. Looking back in gratitude minimized the effect of the disgruntled customer's tirade and gave Mandy the grit to carry on.

Looking ahead means reconnecting with hope of a future goal being accomplished. What does it look like, sound like, feel like? Looking ahead with hope has also been shown to foster grit.

This can be especially helpful after a failure. As a performance for Ben ended, he felt awkward joining the curtain call. He had forgotten a critical line in one scene, stumbled over a piece of scenery in another, and sneezed in the middle of the play's most tender moment. About the only thing that didn't go wrong was not literally breaking a leg. He sighed, joined the cast, and took his bows. Then, behind the curtain, he collapsed onto the sofa still on the stage.

Footsteps from stage right brought the director into his view. Ben braced for the worst. "Hey, rough night, right?" said the director. Ben nodded, putting one hand over his eyes. "Look," continued the director, "you can have a bad night. It's live theater, so anything can happen. But we don't dwell on it because there is always another performance ahead." Ben sighed. "It's fine to feel like tonight was not our best, but the next one could be. Learn from tonight, but think about that next performance." Ben thanked her, got up from the sofa, and walked to his dressing room.

He realized that tonight's mistakes were unlikely to be repeated. With that thought, he began to look ahead. He pictured himself saying the critical line, striding smoothly onto the stage, and not getting a tickle in his nose at the worst possible time. He imagined giving his best performance yet. He started to smile. Soon the hope of what lay ahead renewed his energy and determination to walk on stage the following night.

Look back in gratitude and forward in hope. Repeat your mantra. Quiet that brain enough to have that important "calm conversation."

Soon you will be pressing on rather than pushing the stop button on pursuing your goals. But to do this, you need to practice.

The concept of "How you practice is how you play" is true for more than just artists and athletes. It can become part of your mental game too. The choice is giving in vs. grit, resignation vs. resilience, and throwing in the towel vs. rising up in hope. Grit can define all of us. But we have to practice deliberately and prepare the mind. We have to aim our thoughts in the right direction. Why? Because the body cannot outperform the mind, relationships cannot outgrow the mind, and achievement cannot outpace the mind. Practice now so you can find grit the next time you need it.

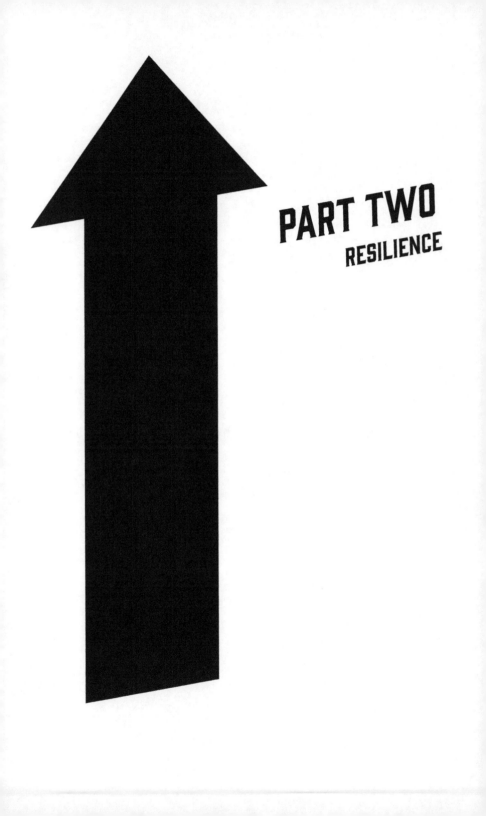

PART TWO
RESILIENCE

CHAPTER 5
THE PRACTICE

Life is not about how fast you run or how high you climb
but how well you bounce.
— Tigger

I love Super Balls. As a school child I loved watching these orbs of synthetic rubber bounce and bounce and bounce. (They were especially fun in classrooms where the teacher had stepped out into the hallway for a moment.) Thrown with any oomph at all, a Super Ball bounces back with force. According to its Wikipedia page, Super Balls have been *bounced* over three-story buildings. Small spheres that come back from a downward trajectory to reach higher heights—that's resilience!

For those of us formed from more down-to-earth materials, bouncing back is more difficult. When we're thrown down, we feel like it's easier to stay put than to reach for further heights. Who wants to bounce when settling in is comforting, cozy, and safe?

You do. In your heart, you know that resignation and surrender are not the route to achievement, confidence, and happiness. Getting to those desirable places requires resilience.

Resilience is the name we've given to the ability to respond positively and grow through adversity. While grit is what we need in a moment of crisis, and a learning mindset is what we need following success or failure, resilience is what we can cultivate as an enduring element of character.

Resilience is:
- a choice, not an ability
- an intertwined combination of grace, grit, and hope
- a willingness to respond to conditions with shifting definitions of success
- a determination to talk one's self back into a mindset that is eager to learn
- an embrace of process en route to outcome
- a desire for community, not company
- a collection of strategies that become more easily and naturally applied with practice, providing the mental agility necessary for bouncing back

Resilience is not a fixed trait. No one is always resilient. Instead, it is a process that resists the notion of defeat and surrender in favor of sustaining renewed focus and effort. Initiating this process begins with a choice.

What You Decide

Like grit, we talk about resilience as if it's genetic. Some people won the lottery at birth, and the rest of us didn't. That's not how it works. It is a component of one's character—an aspect that can be cultivated.

Imagine you've been training for years for a meaningful achievement. You've put in the hours of rehearsing. You've planned, prepared all your gear, and are ready to go. The time comes and you confidently begin what you've practiced. What happens when the show goes off the rails?

For example, Vivian prepares for weeks. Her presentation to the board could influence the future of her idea. Her team thinks it is a valuable strategy. Her supervisor sees it as a benefit for the university and arranged the board presentation. Vivian takes a deep breath, steps to the head of the conference table, and begins.

And it just goes wrong. What options do Vivian and you have at this point? Take a moment and list any that come to mind.

If you identified more than one option, you have a choice. At the most basic level, you can choose to succumb, stew in disappointment, and spend your idle hours streaming movies. Or you can choose to reflect on your performance, renew your strength, revise your plans, and return to work. It's an either/or arrangement, which means you get to choose. If hope is the fuel of uprising, choice is its launch code.

Picking yourself up is hard. Emotionally and physically, you may be drained, feeling empty. It's never easy to make the best decisions in such conditions. (Consider how much easier it is to justify junk food when you're hungry.) Feeling disappointed after a setback does not mean you lack resilience—even Super Balls have a moment of ground contact that temporarily reshapes them—but settling into that disappointment and justifying not making any further effort is the definition of failure.

Now, it needs to be said that there are times to quit. The athlete who suffers a career-ending injury may never make it back to the playing field. That does not mean the athlete lacks resilience. Likewise, the businessperson who decides that retirement will provide new opportunities does not lack resilience for not returning to the office. There is a time and season for everything.

How do you know when it is time to quit?

If you are putting your health, either immediate or long-term, at risk, it may be time to stop. Few things are worth reducing your time on earth or your quality of life. This is a judgment call you have to make. We've all heard the stories of individuals who accomplished something significant after being told they'd never walk again or had only a few months to live. The reason these stories make the news is because they are the exception, not the norm. Is the damage you might incur greater than the joy of the pursuit? Is the possible accomplishment worth the discomfort or pain you might endure during or after your preparation and attempt? What do your trusted medical sources suggest? Sometimes quitting is more about keeping what you have rather than risking what you might lose to gain what you don't.

As humans, we develop throughout our lives, and our interests change. Vera Wang went from figure skating to fashion design. Stan Lee wrote his first comic book at age 40. At 76, Grandma Moses discovered an interest in painting. Harrison Ford was a carpenter before he was Hans Solo and Indiana Jones. We grow. We change. Sometimes quitting or reducing the time we spend on one thing is about making time for something else that we find more rewarding.

Short of such dramatic changes, when it's not yet time to quit, we can choose resilience. Stop thinking it's a superpower that you are or are not born with. Instead, look at the options; you have a choice.

Grace, Grit, and Hope

When we encounter setbacks, we have to extend grace to ourselves because forgiveness influences how we define ourselves. Since I didn't achieve what I hoped to, am I a failure? Or am I a person who failed because he tried? Grace says the second. Why are we slow to give ourselves credit? Because we allow how others view us—or how we think others view us—to distort our perceptions. My parents said I was not as good as my sibling. My boss suggested I was not cut out for the job. My teacher said I would never succeed at this. Our thought processes place too much value on negative feedback and comments, often at the cost of remembering anything good that was said. We condemn ourselves by withholding the grace we might extend to others.

Without grace, the condemning voices win. Find the grace to allow your viewpoint to be: I'm a person who occasionally fails because she tries, but I'm also a person who believes that trying and failing is better than surrender and status quo. Remember: grace lays the groundwork for grit and provides the launchpad for hope.

Shifting Success

Many coaches will help a runner prepare for a big race by discussing A goals, B goals, and C goals. An A goal is what the runner strives for if everything goes right. The weather is good for running, the runner feels good, and the nutrition plan works as intended. A B goal is a runner's default if the A goal slips out of reach. Perhaps the day is too warm and humid for an ideal performance, or the runner wakes up that morning with a stuffy head. As you might guess, a C goal is what the runner will still view as success if goals A and B evade him. It's warm and humid, the runner didn't sleep well, and his nagging ankle injury flared up walking to the start line. While it may seem like the coach is creating an excuse for the runner, the approach is actually the opposite. The coach is creating multiple pathways to success.

I even tell my runners that a D goal should not be off the table. Goal D is how the runner will define success when everything goes wrong or something unexpected occurs. Perhaps the runner steps awkwardly jumping from the street to a sidewalk on part of the course. Suddenly, some muscle objects and prevents the runner from continuing to jog smoothly. Goals A, B, and C are now impossible. It's not anyone's fault, it's just the fickle nature of fate. Now what? Step off the course and quit? Perhaps. Or, if the runner feels like continued effort will not cause further injury, just enjoying the rest of the race may become the goal.

Does changing to Goal D indicate the runner failed? Only if you think finishing a race in a less than ideal conditions is a failure. It is just not the success the runner hoped for.

Wait, you might be thinking. What about standards? I agree. We should strive for Goal A every time. But we should not tie our definition of success to only our most lofty goals.

Let's say that you want to write about your childhood. Sharing stories about growing up has always entertained your friends. When one of them suggests that your anecdotes would make a great memoir, you wonder if you could possibly write one. You decide to try. A family event is just three months away, so you target that date for having a completed memoir. It would be fun to share the writing with the people who know the "characters" of your early life.

At first you struggle. Writing is not the same as oral storytelling, and the words do not flow as easily. Then a conversation with a friend produces an idea. Weekly sessions with him via an internet conferencing platform give you an audience, and your tales once again gain entertainment value. Your friend laughs, sighs, and shows surprise at all the right places. After each session, your friend pushes a button and generates a transcript of your story.

With the raw material now on the page, you begin to revise. You discover quickly that this is also different from storytelling. Laboring over word choices, sentence structures, and paragraph breaks is all new to you. Yes, you wrote your way through college, but this is different from a report on the influence of artificial intelligence on artistic expression. While you can tell your friend one story a week, revising that story requires more than the seven days between sessions.

On the day of your family event, you only have three chapters that you feel are ready to share. You take these with you, and your family loves them. Many ask for copies. At one time during the event, your cousin calls across the room to his sister, "Come here! You've got to read this!" The response motivates you. Maybe it is worth continuing to work on the remaining chapters. You know you have at least one group of interested readers.

So, you go back to work. It takes four more months of steady effort, an hour or so each evening after work, but you finally have a complete manuscript.

Are you a failure because it took four more months to achieve your goal? Or what if you completed 90% of your goal but found that last story too difficult to write well? It's different in tone from the rest of your anecdotes, so you choose to leave it out of the completed manuscript. Does accomplishing 90% of your initial goal mean you failed? I certainly would not see it that way. While completing the manuscript in three months may have been ideal, you still had several successes. You wrote and revised consistently for several weeks. You had the opportunity to share your writing with family members. You discovered a new form of expression that you enjoy. There are many things to celebrate despite not reaching your goal.

You can find some element of success to recognize in whatever work you do. This does not mean that everyone writes a book, wins a client, or deserves a trophy, but what did not work tends to blind us to what did. Goal A may have slipped away, but that does not mean that other achievements weren't won.

When the success you want escapes your grasp, adjust your goal. Revise as necessary. Remember, you only fail when you give up.

Return to Learning

Even when you get to celebrate accomplishing Goal B or Goal C, Goal A is still your gold standard. And most likely, you will still feel driven to pursue it. That's great!

Part of resilience is having the humility and the curiosity to examine what went wrong or what could be improved. (Success alone does not mean that further improvements should not be made.) Pride, concerns about what others think, worries about how you view yourself, expecting success without growth and effort, impatience—these are the barriers that prevent us from looking back and examining our recent efforts. If we allow these walls to define our perspectives, we ignore the very information that would make us more successful the next time. Remember, researchers claim that when we make mistakes, we are cognitively in a prime place to learn if we are willing to attend to what went wrong.

When I set out to write a book, I thought I could rip it off without much effort. I had an English degree and did a lot of writing in my work. All that training and experience should translate to a worthwhile draft, right? Well…

I submitted my draft to an editor. He reviewed my work and gave me a phone call. (I remember it clearly because I was in the grocery store and had to buy napkins so I had something to write on!) My writing was bloated with prepositional phrases—a bad habit picked up in academic writing. I lacked examples that would clarify concepts for readers. My use of modifiers was excessive. Basically, I had produced a rough draft. A good start that needed a lot of work.

With writing, I spend more time examining what is not working than creating. Once I have an idea, a rough draft flows quickly from my head to my hands and into a document. I always feel good about that rough draft for a day or two. Then I return to the draft and find failure in every paragraph. (Revision is the real work of writing.) I have to plan to revise, multiple times, in my project timetables. Sometimes I have to address major issues, such as clarity, structure, and the addition of examples. Sometimes I tackle minor issues, such as verb choice, prepositional phrase overuse, and unnecessary modifiers. Most of the time I have to address problems at both levels.

I used to hate this process. After all, the prose was clear and beautiful when it left my head. Why wouldn't the initial draft be good enough? An opportunity to work on a project with a professional editor, as well as a lot of reading about how to write well, changed my thinking. I have seen how attending to my mistakes not only improves my writing, it shapes me into a better writer. I will never produce a perfect first draft, but even that stage of the process is better than it used to be. Quitting when the failures on each page are numerous might allow me to feel artificial pride in my accomplishment, but it will never enable me to improve either my product or my abilities.

Don't let red ink defeat you. Examine what went wrong so you can strategize a route to improvement. In the process, you will strengthen more than your performance. You will be better the next time around.

Embrace the Process

Not every goal requires a lengthy period of preparation, but many do. If your only focus is achieving a mammoth goal, your daily progress toward that end will lack joy. Who wants weeks or months of misery for one moment of fulfillment?

More importantly, such a long-range focus can undercut motivation. It's easier to be resilient when you can look forward to your next opportunity to practice, to learn, to develop. Finding joy in the process helps you to bounce back from smaller failures along the way.

In working with teachers to implement new instructional programs, I can tell which teachers will be successful early on. Some resist change with every fiber in their being. The status quo is familiar, requires little work, and can usually be taught with minimal thinking. Those who find contentment in doing as little as possible rarely succeed with new initiatives—and their effectiveness with the status quo is often painfully limited.

Teachers who "get it," who try to understand why they are changing their approaches, are often more successful. Not only do they work hard to develop effective lessons, but they also seek out and value coaching by experts. You would want your children in their classrooms.

A third group frequently determines the inertia of the initiative. These teachers ask many questions. They do not resist change out of hand, but they do not advocate change for its own sake. They want the confidence that comes from knowing the research, understanding the strategies, and having the time and resources necessary to implement successfully. These initial skeptics often become the program's biggest fans if someone is willing to answer their questions. Together with the group that is excited right away, these teachers create a critical mass that sustains the initiative long enough to become the new status quo.

If you are engaged in pursuing big goals, don't hesitate to ask questions. Find out what you need to know so you can get excited about the next step in the process. More information can also broaden options.

This matters, because even during the process, you will stumble. The students will get confused during a lesson. The final intervals of the speed workout will be slower than the target. The aperture of the camera will be off for some photographs. The carrot cake will overcome your resistance. Remember, if you are trying, you will sometimes fail. If you loathe or dread or just flinch from the process, achievement will always feel far away. Motivation will get zapped, and you'll either quit along the way, or put forth so little effort that Goal A will not be a possibility.

Envision working toward a goal like a road trip. Even the newest, most sophisticated vehicle needs to pause to obtain energy in some form. This break in forward motion does not mean you should retreat all the way to home.

Lily's dream destination was the competition dance team. They had the sharpest and most difficult performances, and they placed well at competitions. She practiced for hours in her bedroom, stretching and perfecting the various moves she needed for the audition. She could see her own improvement, and her dance teacher noticed too.

Then, during a class session, she lost track of where she was in a routine, stepped in the wrong direction, and caused a three-dancer pileup. Lily was mortified. How could she have been so stupid? Now, she thought, I'll never make the competition team. At home that night, she went through her usual routine of practicing, but she didn't bother trying to be precise. If she couldn't make the competition team, why bother? Her dream was overwhelmed by her fear of making another blunder. She let one failure get between her and Goal A. She spent her remaining years of dance muddling through rehearsals and never trying harder. She let one mistake steal her happiness.

The answer for Lily and for us is to find ways to enjoy the process. If it involves an activity you enjoy anyway, that's easier. But it's not unusual to enjoy something, such as public speaking, and not enjoy the process, such as outlining main points and developing slides to illustrate concepts. If this describes you, here are a few ideas:

- Challenge yourself. If you have a presentation to develop, tell yourself that you will have your first two points identified before lunch. If you have to memorize the muscles and bones of the foot, approach the task as a speed-memory challenge. Framing your work as a challenge makes it more difficult to give up partway through. For example, Lily could have challenged herself to sharpen one movement in every rehearsal.

- Make the task into a game. This is my secret to grading submissions to online courses. As much as I see the benefits of online instruction, as an educator I do not enjoy it nearly as much as being together in-person with a group of learners. Yes, tools like Zoom help, but most activities are still completed apart from each other. Because of this, grading is critically important; I need to give my students as much feedback as possible so that they have information on which to act. When I find several assignments awaiting my review, I am tempted to go for a run or suddenly find some pressing errands. Instead, I organize the assignments into chunks. Each chunk gets a time limit, which keeps me focused. When I complete the chunk within the timeframe, I get to take a break and do something else for a few minutes. I "win" a break before starting the next round. Crazy stuff like that gets me to the end of the submissions.

  You can use the same framing. Need to develop that third point of a presentation? Make it a game by forcing yourself to include at least three quotes from 1980's pop songs. (You can delete them later!) Need to prepare an explanation of the First Amendment in easy-to-understand terms? See if you can do it in a three-panel comic strip. The game doesn't matter as long as it feels like something you could "win." For example,

Lily could have made every rehearsal an opportunity to identify one tip or principle she could write down, as if she were
collecting fortune cookie tidbits for dancers.

- Celebrate along the way. Did you nail that speed workout?
Meet a friend for lunch to celebrate. Did you finish developing the presentation? Go to a coffee shop to enjoy your favorite beverage while you begin reviewing your notes. Exceeded
your goal for the number of words you wrote today? Take a
break and watch an episode of your favorite show. Marking
small successes helps you maintain a positive attitude. Lily
could have complimented at least one other dancer after every
rehearsal. Making someone else smile is a mini-celebration,
and it will bring a smile to your face too.

- Mark your progress in graphic form. Remember the days
when you marked progress toward some goal by coloring in
a spot or adding a star to a chart? Research shows that such
a visual approach works beyond elementary school. If there
are identifiable steps you need to complete to achieve your
goal, list them in a flow chart, for example, and then color
in a spot as each step is completed. Making yourself aware
of your own progress fosters motivation for continuing. For
example, Lily could have tracked the rehearsals in which she
noticed improvement in herself. Every improvement would
have added a tally to her chart.

Community, Not Company

I love taking my laptop to a Starbucks and working for a few hours.
I enjoy being with people but only interacting when I want. I have
the company of people without the distraction of conversation. This
penchant is not surprising, because we all are social creatures.

When it comes to bolstering hope, I have always questioned the "you need a community" idea. I have long felt I am self-reliant enough not to need the messiness that comes with seeking support. I find my way to accomplish my goals alone; after all, I am the one doing the work. On the flip side, I am well aware that, on my lonesome, I have allowed my disappointments to stew inside. Without advice you can remain stuck in your misery.

The input of other people in your life is a two-edged sword. Well-meaning words may spur you into action, but they may also raise obstacles that cause you to sink back into inaction. For example, let's imagine that you and I are good friends. You meet me at Starbucks one day and tell me that you have a great job offer in a faraway city. The selfish me can think to myself, "Oh no, I don't want this to happen. Our friendship will definitely change." And if that negative thought dictates my response, I will start asking questions or telling you information that will fuel any fears and uncertainty you have. I may tell you about a relative who lived in that area and constantly complained about the cost of auto insurance. I might recount a news story about a horrific crime that happened in that city. After I go home, I may send you internet postings about poor public schools, a corrupt city council member, and the traffic congestion problems that commuters face.

I am feeding you with fear. I am hoping you will wallow in inaction. I want you to maintain the status quo—because that's good for me.

Fear motivates us *not* to do something. This can be good for you. If you think that green-tinged piece of meat looks scary, you probably will not eat it. Think that loudmouth in the restaurant looks bigger than you? You probably will not confront him. Inaction can save you a headache, but it can also prevent you from moving forward.

Now, let's reimagine our coffeehouse conversation with the positive me. I start asking you questions about the offer and what excites you about the possibility. I tell you that I will miss you greatly, but that I have heard wonderful things about the city. My brother took his children to a museum there and described it as one of the best family occasions they ever had. I bring up the subject of the universities there and how they are involved in important research related to your career field. I mention that even the city's baseball team seems not to be tanking lately.

I am instilling you with hope. I am nudging you away from fear and toward action, to seriously consider the offer.

Obviously, a good friend might do a bit of both, identifying both positive and negative aspects to help you reach a good decision. But look at the differences this can make when you are trying to accomplish a goal. Imagine I nudge you toward hope in these situations:

You tell me you are applying for a part-time job that's very different from your pre-retirement experience.

You tell me you want to get into better physical shape.

You tell me you want to get your paintings into a public exhibition.

You tell me you want to try reconciling with your estranged sibling.

Someone who is just company for you may not respond in a way that drives you toward hope, but a community will. And hope inclines us toward action.

What constitutes a community? Here is my definition: a community is at least one other person who leaves you more hopeful than you were before. Even if you have only one person but you know they have the best of intentions, you have a community.

How did I come to this understanding? After all, I think the company of caffeinated strangers is sufficient. It happened when I came to know a person who inspired my thoughts about community.

A few years ago, I was contacted by a minister who lived an hour away from me. He said he wanted to run in a local 5k race, but he did not want people in his hometown to know he was training. If he ended up quitting, he didn't want to answer the inevitable questions.

Greg not only went on to be a competitive runner in his age group, but also became a close friend of mine. As a pastor, he excelled at building community. He would create unique events, and he enjoyed visiting people in the hospital.

I asked him once how he comforted people who were hospitalized and facing tragic diagnoses. He said, "You don't have to say anything. You just have to be there." Greg followed the same practice when it came to running. Prior to his joining our group, a small group of us would go on long training runs. We all enjoyed the opportunity to chat a bit while running, but that was really it. I knew each member of the group, but I don't think any of us felt more hopeful as a result of running together. Greg's presence changed that. In the first place, he drove more than an hour each Saturday morning to run with us. Infected with his joie de vivre, we became excited about pursuing goals and truly rejoiced when one of us was successful. Greg loved to celebrate and never missed an opportunity to lure us to a bakery for a communal "Woohoo!"

When he passed away suddenly, we all continued to run together, but at least for me, the running felt numb. I put one foot after another, but nothing resulted other than a few calories burned. Once the worst of the grief passed, our little community rediscovered each other. One of the group wanted to try running another marathon. I committed to following his training program so that he would have support on his long runs. Perhaps, as seen in retrospect, I hoped that I would rediscover the community I felt we had lost. And it happened. After these runs and our lengthy interactions, I began feeling more and more hopeful. And that hope sparked action. I began to train for my own return to a marathon.

I would like to say my return to the marathon was a glorious success. It wasn't. But I have never lost hope that the next time it could be. Why? Community.

Company may distract you for a time with conversations that occupy your mind, but community sustains you and keeps you moving. Find a person or group that fortifies your hope. Be that person for others.

Supporting Resilience: Imagination

Toolboxes are interesting snapshots of a person's life. My wife, a photographer, loves taking photos of toolboxes, especially "vintage" ones. They indicate the care an individual has taken in the handiwork, suggest the types of projects that have been tackled, and even imply the owner's priorities.

My own toolbox would show you that my household repair skills are limited. I have the basics—hammers, pliers, a few vise grips, and probably more sound system–specific tools than one person should have. (See, you can infer some of my priorities!) Some tasks require very specific tools, while others can be undertaken with a few common implements. Resilience is a collection of both types—strategies for specific moments and strategies for living in general. We will examine both types in the next chapter, but let's begin with a couple supporting practices.

Resilient people are imaginative.

Imagination enables you to envision what does not yet exist. With highly resilient people, the ability to imagine happens almost by default. When reality is overtly negative, resilient individuals rise above it by imagining what could be. This does not mean that they deny reality and live in the clouds, but that they know where to go to find hope. They recognize that their current reality does not have to define their future.

People who have been forced into solitary confinement but remained psychologically intact often describe how this works. When the depressing surroundings do not change, the only way to avoid fixating on them is to give imagination free rein. This does not mean becoming delusional and eventually psychotic. Bouts of imagination lift your spirits by helping you rise above your current conditions, such as during the work week, that feel restrictive.

You will hopefully never experience solitary confinement, but circumstances can seem to imprison us. I know, because I am slow to activate my imagination sometimes. When circumstances wrestle me to the mat, I get stuck thinking that I'll be pinned forever. What you need to do in such times is imagine what could be. Not only does that lift your spirits and spark some motivation, it also can help you engage in problem solving rather than feeding a victim mentality.

By imagining what could be, you begin to explore how you could get there. At first this may be nothing more than magical thinking, but keep at it long enough, and you will begin to develop a plan. For example, in the earliest stage of writing this book, I went through a lengthy period of believing I didn't have time to write. I had drafted a few chapters that sat untouched for months. I was stuck, not with writer's block, but in the feeling that my circumstances would not change. I accepted that the project was doomed because, even though I was interested in it, I would never have the opportunity to see it through.

When lamenting about it to a friend, he told me a story about Thomas Mann, the 1929 Nobel prize-winning author. He wrote for only one hour every day. I was then challenged to do the same. My friend effectively said, "Your current reality does not have to be permanent. Others have found ways to push forward. Imagine yourself doing something similar." Now, I haven't been able to write for one hour every day, but I am writing much more often. That spark of imagination freed me from the confinement of accepting the status quo.

Feeling trapped by circumstances? Find a quiet place where your mind can play with possible futures. If nothing else, you will escape the stress of feeling like you lack control. Given a chance to let your mind roam free, you may find yourself responding with resilience rather than resignation.

Supporting Resilience: Perspective

I find watching my wife photograph entertaining. One time we were in upstate New York for a race. We walked from our hotel to pick up my race packet a few blocks away. My wife, camera in hand, stood by as I got my race bib and paused to read all the humorous running-themed T-shirts for sale. On the way back to the hotel, we were chatting when suddenly I realized I was not getting any response. My companion wasn't there at all. I looked behind me and saw her lying on the pavement in front of an historic (but still active) firehouse. She wanted a photo that would capture a highly vertical perspective of the architecture. That required a different position—being horizontal on the cement.

Perspective is a powerful influence. What you focus on is shaped by the breadth of your viewpoint. In particular, if you step away from the immediate, you can see the bigger picture. You look beyond your struggles or failures of today. Instead, the overall map of your plan is where you should focus. Lying down on a sidewalk to look skyward is optional.

Ava paused to lie down on her couch and think. The office meeting that morning had been a disaster. Colleagues blamed one another for the loss of a significant marketing contract. Even though their research showed increased brand recognition, the client was dissatisfied with slow profit growth. Ava's job was to lead the conversation so that shortcomings in their work with the client could be identified and an improvement plan could be generated. Ava sighed deeply. The meeting had created more problems than it solved.

"Wait a minute," Ava said to herself. "I need to do exactly what we were supposed to do in that meeting. I need to review the meeting and figure out where things went off the rails." She began replaying the sequence of interactions in her head, looking for places where her intervention might have refocused the conversation. As her perspective shifted from what happened to how it happened, and then to how it could be different, Ava formed a plan in her mind. An hour later, she drafted an email to send to her colleagues the next morning. A new meeting would be scheduled, and Ava knew better strategies for focusing the conversation. A shift in perspective did more than lift her spirits. It equipped her with tools for trying again.

How can you use reflection like Ava did to shift your perspective? First, take the time to pause and ponder what happened. That may require getting away from others for a period of time, or, if talking things through is helpful, getting together with a hope-building friend. I find running to be a great opportunity for reflection, but sitting apart with a notebook and pencil is often just as effective. Whether you are moving, still, or engaged in conversation, the key is to focus your mind on the recent event, whether it was successful or a setback.

Some find contemplating questions to be helpful in targeting their thinking. First, consider the event and its outcome: How did the event and its outcome compare to your expectations? Be specific in your answers. You may feel like everything went wrong, but that's probably not true. Identify what did work even if the result did not meet your pre-event expectations.

Next, focus on what was within your sphere of influence: What was under your control before and during the event? Again, be specific. When things go wrong, we can over-blame ourselves if we're not careful. Doing so will not shift your perspective in a productive direction.

Third, consider any feedback you have received or pursue some feedback if you haven't received any. Feedback, whether positive or constructive, provides information you may be able to act on. So ask yourself: What does the feedback suggest about areas or details that you should target for improvement?

With these factors in mind, it's time to ask: What could you have done differently to potentially change the outcome? Push yourself to not be limited by binary thinking. As humans, we tend to think in either-or terms. Either the weather will be perfect or it will be a problem. Either the event will be a success or a failure. I can improve the next event by either Choice A or Choice B. One way to break out of this two-fold, too limited thinking is to adopt a both-and focus.

If the event could be improved next time by either choosing a new location or by defining specific spaces for certain activities during the event, how could you do both? And with both, what new possibilities are created? Push yourself to think broadly and to combine ideas that lead to new possibilities. If you can only identify an either-or option, keep thinking.

Finally, direct your thinking to new plans or strategies: What do you need to do now? And what do you need to do in the future? Are there actions you can take now to improve the outcome that disappointed you? For example, if you made a presentation that seemed to fall flat, can you create a one-page document to reiterate your main points and send it to the event's participants? Then, as you think about the next presentation, are there better ways you can structure the ideas, or stronger examples you can use to illustrate ideas, or specific graphics you could add to emphasize the ideas? Again, avoid binary thinking. Perhaps a different structure, stronger examples, *and* specific graphics are needed. The key is to identify specific actions you can take as you prepare for the next time. Having a plan will help shift your perspective, and that will enable your productivity, and that will likely improve the outcome next time.

Supporting Resilience: Growth

Resilience is the ability to experience growth resulting from challenges. It's more than bouncing back to the same level. It's soaring past previous levels to discover or achieve new heights.

Resilience-related growth often happens in one of five areas: discovering and taking advantage of new possibilities; finding greater meaning and purpose in one's outreach and actions; understanding personal strength through increased self-awareness; deepening interpersonal relationships; or heightening feelings and expressions of gratitude.[1]

Discovering and taking advantage of new possibilities often involves lateral movement—redirecting energies from one field of interest to another. It may be a closely related field, or it may be an entirely different one. For example, a nurse practitioner discovers an interest in writing, and his experience of treating patients with chronic pain informs his essays. An IT specialist sees a posting from an aviation museum hiring new docents, and her lifelong love of military history suddenly has an outlet. A teacher notices an advertisement for dog training franchises and moves from two-legged to four-legged students.

Similarly, unmet achievements in one sport may prompt an athlete to find another sport in which they can develop and excel. In one heartening example, Vonetta Flowers was a standout sprinter and long jumper during her years at the University of Alabama in Birmingham. She hoped to make the summer Olympic track and field team, but when she failed to make the cut, she made a move. Did she become a track coach? That would have been a predictable move, but no. Did she take up speed walking and attempt to make that summer Olympic team? Again, no. She turned her attention and energy to bobsledding and the winter Olympics. In this new sport, she found a way onto the team and onto the medal stand. In the 2002 games, she was half of the gold medal-winning team in the two-woman bobsled, and in the process, became the first African American woman to win a gold medal in the winter Olympics. Just because one door may open when another one closes doesn't mean that you won't have to search down alternate hallways.

Finding greater meaning and purpose in one's outreach and actions is both an indicator of resilience and a motivator for continued effort. In fact, meaning and purpose are critical ingredients of intrinsic motivation. Deloris felt driven to help a local charity. She cared deeply about reducing homelessness and helping those currently experiencing this crisis. The annual fundraiser occurred in the fall and raised money by selling tickets to a half-dozen home tours. While seeing the houses of the local upper class always nudged the curious to purchase tickets, Deloris wanted the event to do more. She wanted the event to spark in others an understanding of the issue.

Once the homeowners had agreed to let their houses be used for the event, Deloris followed up and asked their permission to do a bit more. Each eagerly agreed, and most offered to help Deloris carry out her idea.

On the weekend of the event, ticket holders visited the participating properties. As they encountered each room, a placard explained what typically happened there. For example, the dining room placard told about family dinners and holidays, emphasizing the warmth and love the room represented. As the visitors exited the home, they encountered an additional placard outside. "Imagine that the house you just left was yours, and that you just stepped outside of it for the last time. You cannot go back inside. Everything in the house is gone. The vehicle you drove to get here is also gone. As you take the next few steps, think about how you will survive, how you will maintain your relationships, how you will now live without a home and without the resources to secure a new one. This is the challenge of homelessness…" The placard continued with a few more lines about typical struggles that a newly homeless individual my face. When the participants returned to their cars, they found a postcard with a QR code that would take them to the charity's website.

Deloris knew that the event offered an opportunity to add meaning and significance to the experience participants would have. And that added meaning sparked added generosity. The event raised 30% more than it had in the past. Find meaning in your efforts, and new achievements may be possible.

Understanding personal strength through heightened self-awareness increases confidence, which provides additional guidance for future efforts. In 2022, I registered for a writers' conference. Every time I heard someone describe me as a "writer," I had every feeling associated with imposter syndrome, and I had no idea what to expect from a writers' conference. But there I was, sitting around a conference table with the other members of the nonfiction group.

Some of them were poets. Some were working on memoirs. Some were already published authors, providing insight and guidance for their readers. Each of us was assigned a half day on which our writing would be the group's focus. During that conversation the one rule was: the writer could only listen, not participate in, the interaction. I was given the last day, which gave me the tormenting feeling of slowly peeling a week-old bandaid off one's leg.

Adding to my discomfort as the day approached was the other author whose work would be discussed the same day. This skilled writer composed some of the most beautiful literary essays I have ever read. The command of language and the ability to express deep ideas and to capture meaningful moments had me not wanting the essays to end. Naturally, he went first.

The chapter you are reading is the chapter I took to the conference. So, after reading a literary essay, the group read my first sentence. In case you've forgotten what it is: "I love Super Balls." I felt like we had gone from the full potential of language to move readers to the depths of trite pablum. And now I had to remain silent as these skilled authors talked about my attempt with self-help writing. I had no idea that a life-changing event was about to happen.

Interspersed among the recommendations, such as adding a section on knowing when to quit, were positive comments. Some of my ideas were good. The section on community sparked interest and insight. The bittersweet nature of some sections was recognized. Like the Super Ball, I was about to bounce back with a new identity. By the end, I could not wait to get back to work. Why? Because I *am* a writer.

Through my interactions with that amazing group of people that week, I became aware of my own abilities, my strengths and weaknesses. And even though I went into my review feeling completely unnerved, I came away feeling like I could accomplish my goals with this book. I left thinking I was capable of finishing what I started. I discovered an extra measure of resilience, which sparked insight and fueled confidence.

Resilience can also lead to deepened interpersonal relationships. Shared struggles are like magnets: they can pull two people closer or push them apart. Resilience in these situations often results from teamwork. In January of 2019, the St. Louis Blues were in last place with the worst record in the National Hockey League. A humorous encounter with a hit record from 1982—Laura Branigan's "Gloria"— seemed to turn the team around. At every home game, "Gloria" blared over the ice rink during the team's warm-up. And they started winning. Unless you believe the song itself holds mystical powers, something else was going on.

Listening to the players talk about that season, one thing becomes evident: the silly encounter with a decades-old Top Ten hit single brought the team together. They began finding resilience as they worked cooperatively to change their fate. It worked. They won the Stanley Cup that season. To celebrate, several of the players got "Gloria"-related tattoos, and left the season with a championship and with friendships that will last a lifetime.[2]

In summary, resilient people know that they can choose how they respond to setbacks. They examine the different options and pick the one that will lead to learning from mistakes and trying again. They extend grace to themselves so they can begin the work of rebuilding rather than wasting energy on rebuffing themselves. When conditions for an optimal outcome do not exist, resilient people focus their efforts on what good outcomes still are possible. They know that learning, whether they experience success or failure, will enable them to keep growing. Resilient individuals know that the process is more than preparation for single moments—that the process holds its own opportunities for joy and fulfillment. And resilient people are not loners. They find and share hope with a community. They develop their abilities to imagine possible futures and knock down walls that limit their perspectives. Finally, resilient people are determined to grow, finding new avenues, reasons, or relationships that will enable continued progress.

Now, how do we promote such growth in ourselves? How do we become more resilient? How do we develop uprising strength? Seven strategies can prime the mind for physical and professional achievement, relational growth and expansion, and personal improvement. Let's explore them in detail.

CHAPTER 6
THE STRATEGIES

I have learned how to harness the power of perspective; by leveraging a positive outlook, while at the same time being especially mindful of the perilous blind spots of biases and assumptions, it's possible to see how to conquer the unimaginable.
— Brad Snyder

" I knew that there was just no way life could return to normal. One, I'm blind. Two, I couldn't do my job anymore. Three, the foundations of your life, your career, your identity, your family, all that stuff, are really shaken after something like that."[1] The *that* Brad Snyder is referring to happened in Afghanistan. In 2011, while Brad was on deployment as an Explosive Ordnance Disposal Officer, a nearby improvised explosive device blew up. Although thrown to the ground, Brad was basically in one piece—arms and legs were still in place. But all he saw was darkness. The explosion stole his sight, permanently.

Fast forward one year. Brad stands atop a medal stand at the 2012 Paralympic Games, the gold medalist in the 400-meter freestyle. From devastating loss to swimming pool triumph, Brad would go on to win another gold and a silver in the water, and then, because swimming was apparently not challenging enough, he switched to the triathlon and won America's only gold medal in the event in either the Olympics or Paralympics.[2]

What does a person do to find such resilience? What moves the mind to hard-earned performance, well-paced achievement, and strengthened relationships? What can we do to develop this virtue in ourselves? Seven habits can help.

Practice 1. Start with the Positive

When the inevitable challenging times come, train yourself to identify everything you have in your favor. This initial positive interpretation calms your mind and enables strategic thinking.

Author Eric Barker[3] relates a story that illustrates the power of positive first thoughts. A bomb disposal expert in the Navy once attempted to diffuse an underwater explosive. During the dive something went wrong and the officer found himself trapped with both hands and feet entangled. Now, I don't know about you, but if ever there was a time to panic... That's not what he did, however. His first thought after realizing his situation was, "I'm still breathing, so that's good. Now what else do I have that's going for me?" Yes, he was trapped (reality), but nevertheless, he could take advantage of positives (still breathing).

As part of this positive pause, he realized his fingers were still free to move. He thought, "If you can wiggle your fingers, the line that's wrapped around you [may be untangled from your hand]...if you can do one little thing to make it a little bit better, then do that." Obviously, he lived to tell the story, so one small step led to another until finally he was free. The officer describes this approach as "cascading positivity." Yes, this was an emergency, but his predicament would remain dire only if he could not find a solution. By starting with the positive, he was able to problem solve rather than panic. Panic destroys your capacity for self-help, whereas problem solving reveals steps you can take toward solutions.

It's easy to focus on what is working against you. However, doing so, especially if these are factors you cannot control, only steals energy that could be used for problem solving. When you start from a place of resilience, you can shift to another perspective and devote energy to identifying tools you can use to move forward.

To do this, be mindful of your outlook when facing a challenge. Catch yourself slipping into the negative and intentionally redirect your thoughts. Practice this enough and you will eventually find that a more natural response to difficulty is starting with what is working for you.

Practice 2. Express Gratitude

We examined gratitude as a route to grit in Chapter 3. Being thankful promotes feelings of security, trust, and connectedness. These feelings steer you away from stress toward a relaxed state, which provides a home ground for positive perspectives.

Being more grateful requires greater awareness and the intention to act on it. Look for opportunities to express gratitude to others. Thank the barista who brightened your morning with the perfect cup of java. Thank the person at home who made you lunch or mowed your lawn. Send thank-you notes to individuals who recently helped you or gave you a gift. Keep a journal where you list what you are thankful for each day. Promote an attitude of gratitude in yourself by consciously looking for opportunities to express thanks. Altruistic action fosters a positive perspective.

Here is an example of how this works in practice. Harper struggled with occasional feelings that life had passed her by. When she shared this with a close friend, she was asked when she felt this way. At first Harper didn't know, but then she realized that it was usually after spending time on social media. "Oh," said the friend. "That will do that to you—make you feel like everyone else has a better life. Most people only post their best moments, so it can seem like they are living the dream." Harper thought about this and announced that she would take a break from social media for a few days. "That sounds wise," said her friend. "What will you do with those minutes you would normally be scrolling online?" Harper wasn't sure.

Later that afternoon, she heard a news report about a man who wrote one thank-you note every day. Sometimes the recipient was someone he remembered fondly, such as his sixth-grade history teacher. Other times he wrote to someone he just encountered that day, such as an attendant at his gym. Harper liked the idea. She phoned her friend and committed to writing at least one thank-you note each day.

At first the choices were easy—parents, former teachers, close friends—and then the selection process became more challenging. Harper had to start looking for people to thank. And as she did, she felt her own happiness expand. She noticed she had an increased tendency to thank people in person. She became discouraged less often and bounced back faster than she had previously.

In addition to resilience, gratitude has been shown to foster better sleep. Individuals who keep journals where they list at least three things they are grateful for at the end of each day fall asleep faster and sleep more soundly through the night.[4] Increased rest also supports greater resiliency.

Practice 3. Nurture Relationships

Individuals who can identify close friendships in their lives have support beams for building resilience. First, they are better at coping with stress. Friendships anchor us and help us keep a healthy, positive perspective. If you are miserable, a good friend won't let you remain in that state.

This past summer, I experienced knee pain that would not go away. When I went to my physical therapist for answers, he immediately got me in to see an orthopedic doctor. After x-rays, the diagnosis was osteoarthritis. This was definitely not the news I hoped for.

I wallowed in misery, announcing that all my goals in running were no longer attainable, even though the doctor had told me to keep running. Life, as I had known it, was over, I whined to anyone who would listen. My Saturday morning running mate would have none of it. Jack listened for a while and then said, "Nah, you've got a lot more running still in you."

Boom! A reality check. Hearing him say it helped me believe it, and I began to problem-solve rather than complain. I've been running for several months since that conversation. When you can't find resilience on your own, a friend can help you rediscover it. Find these friends! Be these friends! Love may move mountains, but friendship can move minds.

Second, people with close friendships are more likely to grow through experience. Just as they provide needed reality checks, friends also share in your experiences—directly or indirectly—and, as a result, can help you process the events. They can provide an empathetic ear, but they also can provide helpful input.

My wife and I both have activities apart from our work that we not only enjoy, but that enable us to influence the world in creative ways. However, work tends to swallow our time, even on the week-ends—especially when both of us work out of home offices. During a recent break we both expressed our frustration with how rarely we got to pursue these passions—photography for her, writing for me—and how we both also wanted to remain fit. My wife posed a possibility: what if we flipped our normal daily schedule by starting with the things we wanted to pursue and then beginning our work day? We discussed it and decided to give it a try. So far this change has been great. We both feel better about our lives, and are even more thoughtful in our "day jobs." Shared experiences led to helpful input that improved our lives.

Third, friends can motivate healthy responses to a challenge. Specifically, friends can stoke intrinsic motivation. They do this by helping us to see which options we have, and by helping us believe that we are capable of something more. More than inspiring, they help us direct our thoughts and energies.

Liam felt like his supervisor was constantly picking on him. Even when Liam tried his best, the boss would make comments about how something could have been done quicker or with better results. When venting his frustrations on a Friday night, a friend asked him what was good about the job. Liam thought a minute and then said that he liked the tasks he got to complete and he enjoyed his coworkers. "Okay," replied his friend. "So not everything is negative. When it comes to working with your supervisor, what is working in your favor?"

Now Liam really had to pause and think. "Well, I obviously have his attention," Liam realized.

"Okay, what else?"

"I do not have to guess what he's thinking," Liam explained. "He's very direct in his feedback."

His friend nodded. "Tell me about the most recent time he gave you feedback."

Liam detailed how he had completed a task carefully. He emphasized how his supervisor had walked past while he was working on the task but didn't give negative feedback until it was finished.

"Okay, let's break that down," suggested Liam's friend. "You have a supervisor who pays attention to your work, both during and after a task. He's good about giving you direct, clear feedback, but only when it's too late to change the way you are doing it. So, you feel overly supervised and constantly criticized. Is that accurate?"

"Yes," he agreed, "that's it."

"Let me ask you a question," said his friend. "Does the fact that he wanders by while you are working suggest anything positive to you?"

Liam's first thought was, "No way!" His friend was serious, though, so Liam searched for an answer. "Hmm, maybe he's interested in how I'm approaching the task. I'm not really sure."

"Well," retorted his friend, "think about it. He's watching, he's good at offering direct feedback, and you have his attention. So what could you do to turn all of that into a positive experience?"

"Sheesh," Liam thought, "all I wanted was to vent my frustrations, and now I'm supposed to come up with a solution." He considered the question, connecting the details: attention, feedback, process. "Maybe," he started, "I could ask him for feedback during one of his passes while I am working. Then, if he had any, I could act on it immediately. That way I might show respect for his expertise and be able to complete the task in a way that makes him happy."

"There are no guarantees," responded his friend. "But that seems like a strategy worth trying."

Liam couldn't wait for Monday. Finding what was working, examining a past experience to learn from it, and responding to the challenge with a strategy—all the potential had him eager to return to work. Hope, learning, and grit empowered resilience, and all of it was set in motion through a conversation with a friend.

Practice 4. Acknowledge and Focus

Resilience is not a flight of fancy that we use to escape reality. It is how we cope successfully *with* reality. Specifically, resilient individuals know that directing energy toward what is beyond their control is a waste of time. Instead, the resilient acknowledge what they can't change and figure out a way forward. Rather than "Why is this happening to me?" they ask, "Given this situation, what am I able to do?" Their acceptance of reality leads them to find actions they can take.

In a dramatic incident, Delta Goodrem, a multi-award-winning singer and songwriter, woke from a routine surgery to find a nerve in her tongue paralyzed. Complications during surgery were the unfortunate cause. Doctors informed her that the nerve would heal, but it would have to learn to reconnect with its receptors—a process that could take up to a year. As Delta writes, "My sound is my livelihood and I was facing losing that altogether."[5] Video clips of her in rehabilitation sessions reveal the depth of the damage.[6] It would have been easy to despair, give in, and seek out an easier route to income. That's not what she did.

Accepting the struggle ahead, Delta regarded the year as a time of rebirth. "This was my time to be silent and to observe. It was not my time to speak; it was my time to listen…" Time to reflect resulted in Delta's most personal album. It debuted at the top of the Australian charts and received critical acclaim. She did what she *could* do during a time of feeling paralyzed: she wrote. She acknowledged the challenge, felt the frustration, but focused on what was working for her and on what the future could be. Hope despite the circumstances.

Learning—or relearning—to make progress. Grit when success was slow. Added up, it sparked productive resilience.

Reality may not immediately change, but your response to it can. Acknowledge the circumstances, but focus on what is possible. Given the situation, what are you able to do? You may only find small steps that you can take, but that's still progress.

Practice 5. Pursue Fitness

I hesitated to include this section because fitness is often pitched as a cure for everything. However, research on the benefits of physical activity for neurological and psychological health is convincing. In addition to the general feeling of well-being that regular exercise provides, it also equips us for resilience. Think about the physiological responses to exercise: (1) your heart rate increases, (2) your breathing becomes more rapid, (3) you sweat, (4) your muscles tense, (5) blood flow gets redirected, and (6) blood vessels in active muscles dilate. And these are just the responses you may be aware of. Chemical changes also occur within the body.

All of this heightened physical response teaches the body that such a state is not dangerous—that there is no need to worry simply because these physical responses are occurring. In other words, we learn that a heightened physical state is not a reason to panic, allowing us to activate thought patterns that can lead us to resilience.[7]

Fitness also creates an upward trajectory, a momentum that can help us resist downward trends. Find a goal, work to progress toward it, accomplish it, set a new goal. Stick with exercise long enough and this becomes a natural thought pattern. Even when failure strikes, knowing how to react to physical setbacks eases the way to reflect on why the problem occurred and to develop a plan to overcome it on the next attempt. Stick with exercise long enough and the thought patterns around it transfer to new areas of your life. You will find that a failure at work will be easier to overcome with resilience, not (just) because you are more physically fit, but because exercise has trained your mind to bounce back and grow.

Elena's doctor, for instance, suggested she find ways to relax. Her blood pressure and yo-yoing weight indicated that stress was a worrisome factor in her life. She began walking on a nature trail near her home. Her first walk was ten minutes, five minutes out and five minutes back. During those ten minutes Elena found her shoulders relaxing and her breathing slowing. A few days later, Elena walked farther. And a few days later, farther still.

She started carrying a sketchbook with her, walking until she found a detail that caught her eye—an unusual tree, an interesting bird, a scene along a creek. Then she sat down, spent a few moments sketching, and then continued with her walk. In a few weeks, Elena was walking more than an hour, 3-4 times a week. She found the stress at the shipping company where she worked less taxing. She found fresh ideas flowing more freely and made suggestions at work that could lessen the stress for all her colleagues. Her walks in the woods became the launchpad of a better life.

Burning calories and building muscle bolsters the mind. Regular exercise equips us physically and mentally to be more resilient. Training the body also trains the mind.

Practice 6. Find the Funny

My friend Greg, who I mentioned earlier, was a master at finding or providing humor. After crossing the finish line of his first full marathon, Greg's next stop was the medical tent, where two full bags of fluid were streamed into him. We drove back to the hotel, and we took the elevator up to the third floor. While shuffling down the hall, we encountered a housekeeping cart, meaning we had to shimmy our way past it. A few more steps and Greg suddenly turned toward the wall and vomited. In between waves of nausea, he yelled out, "Housekeeping, I'm sorry! Housekeeping, I'm sorry!"

I finally got him to the hotel room, got him seated on a bed, and told him not to move. I turned away, picked up the phone, and called the front desk. When I hung up, I found Greg standing in the middle of the hotel room with his finisher's medal around his neck. "What are you doing?" I said in frustration. With half a smile, he replied, "You have to take my picture so I can post it on Facebook." I couldn't help it. I laughed until I had tears in my eyes. Here he was, after the ordeal of finishing a marathon in very warm conditions, and his major concern was posting on social media.

In addition to being entertaining, his humor lifted his spirits and those around him. How can you dwell in the doldrums when life can be so entertaining?

The uplift that humor brings can change how you view what is ahead. Recently, before my running mate Jack and I ran a marathon, we learned the weather forecast included strong wind gusts. Jack suggested that tracking us could be interesting. "Why is Kevin suddenly moving at 70 miles-per-hour?" Jack joked. That humorous interjection changed my mindset. I hate wind—as has been previously established. But I went into race morning laughing at the wind rather than dreading it.

Humor—not unkind or sarcastic—lifts faces into smiles, pulls people together, and creates conditions in which resilience is more likely. It is a sure way not to take yourself so seriously. If you can pull back the lens and view your situation wryly, you'll be more able to shrug it off and decide how to put it in the past.

Practice 7. Recognize and Avoid the Traps

By now you probably realize that so much of being resilient relies on the thinking patterns you make a habit. Just as you can find healthy approaches to thinking, you should recognize patterns that will pull you in the opposite direction.

One of those traps is personalization. You may find yourself wondering, "Why does this happen to me? Why am I the only one who struggles with this? I must be a failure." This is choosing to define yourself by your failures and wallowing in self-pity. All of these thoughts are lies. Failing doesn't only happen to you, others struggle with the same challenges, and you are not a failure. By allowing these thoughts to occupy space in your head, you are allowing falsehoods to influence your future.

Caleb wrestled with this trap frequently. When he injured his hand during a home-improvement project, he thought, "This kind of screw-up only happens to me." When he was late getting to the airport because of traffic, he ruminated on how complicated his route was compared to everyone else's. Of course, Caleb knew in his head that these conclusions weren't true. He just couldn't prevent having them echo inside his head.

Such thoughts recurred every time Caleb showed up to orchestra rehearsal. He played the cello very well. In both high school and college, he earned first chair in his sophomore years. When he was invited to join a well-respected symphony in his home city, he jumped at the opportunity, expecting to advance quickly to the top of the cello pecking order.

But Caleb started in the third chair. He was stunned but believed he was assigned the lower rank just because he was new. Soon, he'd advance, maybe even be an occasional soloist. When assignments were made the following season, Caleb couldn't believe it. He was still third chair.

Convinced that a mistake had been made, he arranged a meeting with the conductor. She explained to Caleb that he was an outstanding cellist but that he was in a section filled with highly skilled musicians. His skills were not inferior, but his colleagues were equally skilled and more experienced. She encouraged Caleb to keep up his excellent musicianship and remain faithful in adding those skills to the orchestra.

Caleb sulked the whole way home. Once inside his apartment, he called a friend who also played in the orchestra. "This always happens to me and only me," he whined. "It figures that I would get into an orchestra only to find I would never make it to first chair."

"Wait," said his friend. "Who said you would never make it to first chair?"

"The conductor," sighed Caleb. "She said the other cellists were better."

"That's not what you told me," replied the friend. "You told me that she mentioned their experience as a factor in her decision."

"Same thing," said Caleb. "I'll never be as experienced as the rest, so I am stuck, permanently, in third chair. Any other cellist with my abilities would have advanced at least to second chair this year. It's just me and my rotten luck."

"How about we get together for lunch tomorrow?" suggested the friend. "I think there is another way to look at this."

"Fine," Caleb grunted. "It stinks being me, that's all I know. I don't know why I even try."

Whining rarely leads to winning because personalizing failure encourages us to give up. It's *not* just you.

Generalizing is another thought pattern that is an enemy of resilience. You may find yourself thinking, "Well, I failed at this last time, so I will probably fail again," or, "Since I failed in this area, I probably won't be very good in this other area." Again, all these thoughts are lies, but they are powerful enough to become self-fulfilling prophecies. Why should a past failure define what you are capable of the next time? One failure does not have to be a flood that overwhelms all areas of your life.

Diane had the scarring experience of crossing a slalom finish line in last place, even though her time was very respectable. The experience lingered in her mind. For several races after, she feared coming in last. She would say, "I just don't want to come in last." That thought affected her thinking going into every race. "What if I come in last?" Her fear was a stressor that could only negatively influence her performance. Her coach talked a lot about how it was unlikely, how that when it happened she still had a good finish time, how nothing other than her pride was really injured, but the pervasiveness of the thought was tough to overcome.

As she approached the start line, she caught herself spiraling into negative thinking. She told herself to take a timeout. Instead, she started thinking about her home office. One wall held bibs from her races, photos of her in action and with her skiing frenemies, and several of her medals. She had accomplished so much! Why was she focusing on one bad race rather than the joy of racing? Head held high, she positioned herself at the start. Nowadays, she pursues goals with gusto and confidence. She's a better skier, physically and mentally, than she was on that one bad day. Be like Diane: identify pervasive negativity and uproot it from your consciousness. Recognize it as a lie, and look forward with hope.

The third trap builds on the first two: permanence. If you find yourself thinking, "I will never accomplish this. I don't know why I even keep trying," you're stuck in a thought pattern that will defeat you. Again, it's not true. None of us can foresee the future. But we do know that directing our efforts to be better than we are today can lead us to grow. Our current level of achievement does not have to be permanent, unless, of course, we quit trying.

This applies not only to the way we feel about ourselves. We can face repeated setbacks that take on the appearance of permanence. For instance, Phil completed all his Ph.D. classes, earning a B+ or better all the way through. Now all that was standing between him and an advanced degree was a dissertation and its defense. He assembled his proposal quickly, knowing what he wanted to study. However, since his proposed study lacked a method of quantifiable measurement, the Institutional Review Board rejected his proposal. Phil's advisor explained that this was not unusual. He needed to find or develop a tool that could assess what he hoped to measure. Phil researched and found a standardized assessment that he thought would work. He added this to the proposal and resubmitted it.

The board rejected this proposal too. The assessment instrument measured a related element but not what Phil's proposed study focused on. After another round of research, involving an attempt at developing his own instrument for assessment, Phil resubmitted his proposal. In its rejection of the proposal a third time, the board suggested that Phil's instrument could work well, but it needed to be assessed by experts first so that it had some basis for validity.

Frustrated, Phil threw the proposal and the board's notes in the trash. "They're never going to approve it no matter what I do," he complained to his advisor. Despite further encouragement, Phil regarded the committee's rejection as permanent. He quit, accepted a lower degree than he had targeted, and carried the resentment with him for several years. Permanence prompted bitterness, which became blame Phil targeted at others for falling short of his goal.

These are three powerful deceptions[8] that will derail our progress toward resilience. And for several years I struggled with all of them. I would hear the advice that I should control my thoughts rather than letting them control me, but I did not understand how that was even possible. How do you keep such thoughts from crossing your mind? The answer is that you don't. Instead, you treat them as they deserve. Lies merit no respect, no energy, and no room in your head. Try this method instead.

Step 1. Examine your thoughts as if they are items at an auction. Ask yourself, "Would I bid on that?" Remember, if you answer yes, you are committing resources to a subjective view. Don't buy any lies. Treat your thoughts with scrutiny, expose the falsehoods, and change the mental conversation.

One strategy for doing this is to imagine yourself in the place of advisor. Identify the thoughts like, "I'll never get better at this so I might as well quit." Ask yourself if that is advice you would give to a friend. If not, it's not good advice for you either.

Looking *at* thoughts rather than perceiving *from* thoughts enables us to *redirect* thoughts, which can nudge us toward resilience.

Step 2. Reframe difficulties as challenges. Consider the difference between these two statements: (1) *I hit a roadblock.* (2) *I have a challenge.* Do you sense the implicit difference between them? A roadblock can stop us in our tracks. A challenge can be overcome.

In recent years, obstacle course races have become very popular. These events are less of a race than a sequence of physical challenges. You might be crawling under barbed wire one moment, scaling a wall the next, and then trudging through sticky mud the next. In many of these races, you can choose to skip a limited number of challenges, but only with a time penalty added to your finish for each one.

The advice of friends who have completed these races is always the same: treat the event like an adventure rather than a race. Treat each challenge as an obstacle to overcome rather than a block to your progress. Some of the challenges require help from other competitors, some of them require perseverance, and all of them require a sense of humor. Attitude has a bigger influence than physical strength on how they finish.

So, as you stumble over a multi-octave run in a piece of music, regard it as a challenge. As you cross the finish line three minutes behind your target time, view that gap as a challenge. As you read the rejection letter from a potential employer, view the next interview as a challenge. And with whatever challenge you face, keep a sense of humor. Remember: find or be the funny, and view the challenge as something you can overcome.

Step 3. Cultivate hope. This topic has been discussed before, and one idea is worth repeating: the power of the word *yet*. Any time you think about what you can't do, be sure to end the statement with *yet*. For example, I cannot draw a face with the right proportions *yet*. I have not reached my target weight *yet*. I have not widened my social circle *yet*. This three-letter word helps you reframe a difficulty as a challenge, and sparks the hope that with continued work you will be able to accomplish your goal. This is the essence of resilience. Rather than giving up, we encourage ourselves to continue.

Before we plumb the depths of despair and discuss exit strategies, let's examine a few key concepts we've explored so far:

- The body cannot outperform the mind; achievement cannot outpace the mind; relationships cannot outgrow the mind.

Hope
- Hope picks a vision of a possible reality that does not exist yet.
- Focus your hope on a challenging but possible objective.

- Hope focuses and works on making a desired outcome a reality—some planning required.
- Hope perseveres with strategic thinking and a willingness to achieve something other than its initial vision.
- Hope celebrates.
- Hope knows that setbacks and discouragement are temporary.
- Hope sees failure for what it is: feedback.
- Hope thrives within a community who believes in us.
- Hope is the fuel of a productive mindset.

Learning Mindset

- This type of mindset humbly believes that you can improve through strategic effort.
- This mindset provides: grace for error, strategy for improvement.
- Pride makes quitting seem inevitable.
- A learning mindset in one area does not guarantee a learning mindset in another.
- Curiosity is critical for sustained improvement.
- Having the humility and the curiosity to examine what went wrong or what could be improved nudges us toward resilience.
- "Okay, the way I just tried to achieve my goal (swim that race, organize my work, solve that problem) was not successful. Let me see if I can figure out why and how I can change my approach so that I am more likely to be successful."
- While a learning mindset helps us improve following failure (or success), grit keeps us going during our attempts.

Grit

- Grit is a mindset.
- We can choose grit.

- Deliberate practice is intentionally working just beyond your current expertise, abilities, or endurance. Deliberate practice develops grit.
- Grit can be found by bringing your core values to mind.
- You can talk yourself into grit: acknowledge, connect to your values, and reframe.
- Repeating a mantra quiets your prefrontal cortex and boosts dopamine levels in the brain, enabling you to engage the "quiet conversation" that leads to grit.
- Looking back with gratitude and forward with hope sparks grit.

Even as we develop resilience, bad things will happen. Some of them may push us beyond our ability to make resilient choices. We may feel defeated, discouraged, and find ourselves leaning into depression. We may not have the energy to apply these strategies of resilience. Or we may not even want to be resilient because the minimal energy it takes to give up feels good. What do we do then? When our extraordinary strength fails us, how do we find our way back to hope? Let's find out we can escape such a funk.

CHAPTER 7

THE REBOUND

You build on failure. You use it as a stepping stone.
Close the door on the past. You don't try to forget the mistakes,
but you don't dwell on it. You don't let it have any of your energy,
or any of your time, or any of your space.
— Johnny Cash

Remember that race back in Chapter 1 when I called my wife and begged her to track me down and get me out of it? The misery did not end then. I stewed about that race for weeks. The feeling went beyond disappointment and frustration. I sank into a funk that colored all of my thoughts. I was a terrible runner, so I might as well give up. I hated my work and wasn't good at it, so I might as well quit. I was an awful friend because I brought everyone down, so I might as well go it alone. As a failure I had nothing to offer, so I should quit writing and avoid any public speaking. My lack of success in one race meant that I could never be successful again.

I know. It's silly, foolish, crazy, insert-your-own-adjective here. It was one race!

Yet I spent more than three months training for it. I thought a major accomplishment was possible. I had built it up in my head as being "the chance" at checking off an achievement I'd chased for years. That one race zapped all my uprising strength.

A carpenter, Jackson, had a similar slide following a failed woodworking project. His attempt at creative expression only illuminated his limitations as a craftsman. Jackson usually fashioned handmade furniture. This time he had hoped for a unique expression of his own. In frustration, he stomped out of his workshop, slammed the door, and vowed to avoid the place.

For several days the failure led to questioning his abilities, which produced insecurity and sparked doubt in his skill as a woodworker. And that spiraled quickly toward permanent pessimism.

Disappointment left to its own trajectory leads to discouragement, and that left to its own course leads to depression. Now, if you feel that you are depressed (and sometimes friends are better judges of that than we are ourselves), please seek help. Nothing in this book is meant to substitute for the help of an expert. The American Psychological Association has helpful information on its website: https://www.apa.org/topics/depression.

If, like me, you experience only the occasional emotional funk after a disappointment, you can avail yourself of strategies that help.

Feel It

Ignoring a setback and subsequent disappointment only delays your comeback. This includes making up excuses for the setback, because excuses allow you to maintain the status quo, which probably contributed to the setback. As long as you disregard reality, resilience will remain distant. On the other hand, an emotionally honest examination opens you in the right direction. Researcher and writer Diane Coutu[1] puts it this way: "The fact is, when we truly stare down reality, we prepare ourselves to act in ways that allow us to endure and survive extraordinary hardship."

Feeling discouragement can be motivating if you approach it in the right way. While confidence is a positive trait, pride is not. If you examine your failure from a perspective of being too good for the failure to have happened, it will lead to the point of concession. In contrast, examining the same experience from a point of humbleness can motivate you to try—because humility always seeks ways to improve.

However, you don't just want to relive the setback. That's a certain route to deeper discouragement. As you "stare down reality," do so with the idea of finding meaning in it. Our brains naturally create patterns (which is why conspiracy theories can be so attractive). The brain desires meaning, and meaning is the kryptonite of despair.

One way to approach this is to ask yourself what was gained or what you could learn from the setback. Despite the failure to achieve a goal, did you discover that you can persevere in the midst of a challenge? Did you find supportive people who not only understand but can assist you in your next attempt? Does the experience help you know better how to assist others in some way? In addition to identifying how to better approach your next attempt, how is this setback meaningful? Meaning often manifests as an insight. If you find yourself thinking "Aha!" at some point in your review, you've probably mined some meaning.

Reviewing your disappointing performance in this way does more than generate positive feelings about your attempt. It reorients your focus. You are giving yourself permission to dream again, to reimagine a future that sparks hope. "Clear-eyed, hope gives us the courage to confront our circumstances and the capacity to surmount them."[2]

That can help in a matter as simple as pickleball. In the tournament finals Daniela and her partner had won only the runner-up ribbon. In Daniela's mind, that meant they had lost the championship. She ignored any lessons she might take away from the disappointment and tried practicing harder. Her over-the-top practicing was noticed by her partner, mostly because it sparked more mistakes than mastery. After one aggressive error, Daniela's partner suggested they quit for the morning and head to a coffee shop.

Over lattes, they chatted briefly, and then her partner said, "Daniela, what's going on? Why are you practicing with force but not focus?"

Daniela had to question her thoughts. "I'm mad," she mumbled. "We should have won that championship." Her pickleball partner leaned back as Daniela continued. "We lost because of my mistake in the final volley. So, I'm mad at myself, and you should be mad at me too."

"Okay," said her partner, "let's review that final match." Working together, they pieced together how each point had been scored. Then they examined the points they lost. Where were they on the court? How well had they communicated with each other? What was the position of the paddles in their hands? As they analyzed everything, Daniela reached an epiphany.

"On almost every point we lost, we were in the same positions, and the ball was hit into the same area. We just need to figure out how we can position ourselves to close off that lane."

That discovery led to the beginnings of a strategy. At their next practice, the pair worked on covering the court, trying out different positions and noting the results. Eventually, they found a way to defend the lane that had led to their loss. Daniela found concentrat-

The Rebound | 141

ing on a solution refocused her mind on the game. Disappointment became the foundation of improvements.

Feel the disappointment, but do not kill hope in the process. Acknowledge the setback and search for meaning. What have I gained/am I gaining from this experience? Keep searching until you can shout "Eureka!"

Write It Out

Writing is an excellent way to "force" yourself to process thoughts. You have to name your ideas and feelings, and you have to connect concepts. Putting words to your thoughts and emotions gives you a named challenge to overcome. Instead of some vague emotional state you need to move past, you identify issues in black and white that can be addressed. Labeling and sorting your disappointment calms down the amygdala, a structure in the brain that is involved in processing emotions. This enables the right and left hemispheres to communicate more efficiently and to diminish emotional reactions.[3] As writer E. M. Forster put it, "How do I know what I think until I see what I say?"

Research supports the benefits of writing as a means of processing setbacks. Studies[4] have correlated writing with:

- better thinking and improvements in symptoms of long-term diseases, such as irritable bowel syndrome
- lowered blood pressure
- improved mobility in patients with arthritis
- reduced depression and negative thinking
- improvements in specific body parts, such as the lungs, in patients with diseases affecting those areas

Writing is an invitation to take a break. It promotes reflection and relaxation while providing a safe outlet for strong emotions. Mad at yourself for striking a downer note at the end of a speech? Write about it. Irked with a client who chose your competitor despite your better offer and harder work? Let the disappointment flow through your pen or keyboard. Angry with yourself over a lapse following rehab? Reflect and write about it. Writing provides an opportunity to express your thoughts without concern over how they are being received by someone else. Go ahead and "yell." Nobody but you needs to read your screed.

Since writing requires connecting ideas, it can uncover important patterns. For example, you may discover a cause-effect relationship between ideas. Suddenly, you have a very specific issue you can address: the cause. Or you may discover a sequence of decisions or actions that contributed to an outcome. Again, you now have a concrete issue you can tackle. Which step in the sequence tipped the result toward failure? Did a series of choices lead further from success rather than bringing it closer? Writing can help you process where you are and promote a better strategy for moving forward. It aids resilience, calms tensions, and improves outlooks.

Nick's outlook was colored by annoyance with himself. A music competition required him to transpose a piece of music on the spot. The judges handed him the score and told him to play it in F major. He studied the music for a moment before lifting his clarinet to his mouth. He played the entire piece, and it sounded perfect. Except that instead of playing in the key of F, he played in the key of G. His transposing was off by an entire step, and the judges could tell by his finger positions during the piece. They thanked him politely and then called for the next contestant.

Nick knew how to transpose. He knew how to play in F major. How could he have made such a dumb mistake? Stewing in silence as his mom drove him home gave him time to dwell on the error. When he reached his bedroom, he was so upset he could barely think. He flopped into his bed in abject misery. Then he noticed his journal on the nightstand. He sat up, sighed, and picked it up. He wrote a firehose of sentences, filling one page and bleeding over onto the next. Slowly, Nick felt his body relax and his emotions mellow. By degrees he recovered from his funk. From this calmer state, he was able to recognize what happened. At the next competition, he would not make the same mistake. Writing calmed his mind to the point where he could strategize a way forward. Writing nudged him toward resilience. Writing helped him rise up.

Hang Out with the Right Friends

When I am in a funk, the last thing I want is people telling me, "It's not so bad," or, "Look on the bright side!" I realize they are trying to be helpful, but they irritate me and harden my resolve to stay negative. My advice is to avoid such friends until your perspective shifts.

Who, then, should you seek out? First, laughter is a powerful medicine. Spend time with friends who have ways of making you laugh, but not friends who will laugh at you. Laugher at someone's disappointment feels like scorn, which will definitely not help your perspective. Hang out with those who are witty, or who tell great stories, or who always have great jokes. Laughter may be a temporary lift, but any upward movement gets your head moving in the right direction.

In the brain, laughter sparks a release of dopamine, which improves mood. Dopamine also improves your ability to examine important concepts and critical details,[5] creating an ideal mental state for exploring your setbacks and identifying strategies for moving forward. Laughter may prime your brain for insight and strategy.

Time with people who know how to challenge you without making you feel the threat of failure are good companions too. Remember the party that Brad Snyder[6] attended after being blinded by an improvised explosive device in Afghanistan? At that party he found himself surrounded by well-meaning old friends. Instead of being uplifted by the reunion, he "became dismayed by how many of them said that they were sorry, and how they had been so sad to hear the news of my injury." Brad explained that even though he was no longer a guy who jumped out of planes and dismantled bombs, he "didn't want anyone to worry about" him, and he "certainly wasn't seeking out any pity."

In contrast, later at that same party, Brad suddenly heard a "familiar gruff voice." His former swim coach, Fred Lewis, welcomed Brad's emotional hug, and then said, "When are you coming back to practice?" Brad explained: "Fred knew me, and he knew that I didn't want to be pitied. He knew that I had become a warrior, and I just needed a challenge to jumpstart the rest of my life." The next morning, Brad jumped into a swimming pool in order to train for the gold medal he would eventually win. That "gruff voice" helped Brad find uprising strength.

Time with the right friends re-energizes, reorients, and restores hope. The medicine of friendship simply requires time. Give yourself a prescription.

Talk It Out

No, I'm not advising you lie on a couch and pour out your soul. Talking to a friend, or a coach, or a colleague, who can understand your frustration, help you process it, and help you strategize how to move beyond it can be incredibly beneficial.

First, you have more than a listening ear. You have someone who has likely experienced what you have or a similar trial. They are equipped to know both your feelings and the depth of them.

You see such pairings all the time. For example, an email stated that Alexis's essay had not reached the final round of a competition.

It was her best work, and she hoped it would be among the finalists. Months of writing, revising, and editing led to this short, matter-of-fact email. Defeat and discouragement flooded Alexis's thinking. She picked up her phone and scrolled through her contacts.

Yolanda picked up on the second ring. Alexis read her the brief email. Yolanda listened and then suggested they meet for lunch the next day.

Over burgers, Yolanda shared how a few weeks previously, she had submitted one of her best sketches to a local competition. She didn't make it past the first round, and she was deeply disappointed at first. So, she understood Alexis and she had bounced back from a similar experience. As a result, Alexis began to feel more positive.

Second, you are interacting with someone who can ask knowledgeable questions. This can aid in identifying what went wrong or what caused the unfortunate outcome. It also decreases the likelihood of frustrating irrelevant questions from a well-meaning but uninformed friend. Calmly processing your thoughts will move you toward resolution.

To return to the previous example, Yolanda began asking questions. Had Alexis seen any comments from the judges? Did Alexis have any idea of what prevented her essay from progressing to the final round? Alexis said she didn't. Undeterred, Yolanda continued posing questions. Did Alexis know who was on the judging panel for the competition? Alexis answered that their names and email addresses were listed on the competition's website. "Hmm," responded Yolanda. "Have you thought about contacting them?"

Third, such a friend can help you turn the corner and begin strategizing your next move. Hopefully, she will help you envision a possible future, examine the past, and then develop a strategy for what is next. In other words, such a friend can nudge you toward resilience.

Alexis jumped ahead in her thinking. "I could contact them! Maybe at least one of them will give me some feedback I can use." Yolanda smiled and nodded. The sting of the disappointment hadn't disappeared, but it was suddenly less of an influence on Alexis's thinking. Good could come of this, Alexis thought. I can find out how to strengthen that essay further before I submit it for possible publication.

Similarly, at dinner one evening after a full day of conference teaching, Zach and a colleague discussed their experiences. Zach expressed frustration with a series of workshops he led, explaining that his attendance dropped at each successive session and he was not connecting with those who stuck with him. Zach's colleague shared that a similar down trend happened to him one time while leading professional development for a school faculty.

He then began asking Zach questions. What was the physical setup of the meeting room? Was Zach up on a stage behind a podium? How did he structure the workshop? What hints did Zach give about the contents of the next session? While they talked, Zach realized that he had saved the information people really wanted for the final session, rather than scattering tips throughout. He was presenting all the supporting research first, and then hitting all the potential implications for teaching in the last session. People were not getting what they wanted early enough to stay with him.

When he returned home, Zach revamped the workshop series. The next time he led it at a conference, his attendance increased with each session. The teachers asked so many great questions that Zach had to shift the session into the hallway to prevent delaying the next scheduled workshop.

Talk it out with the right person, and you'll navigate toward resilience and closer to a solution.

Move in New Spaces

Getting out of your usual surroundings does more than change the scenery. It can calm your spirit, clear your mind, and change your perspective. Experiences in nature, for example, yield a cascade of benefits. Art museums have also shown to have positive effects. Get out of your known world for a time and immerse yourself in a less familiar place.

I have experienced this burst of refreshment personally. During a phase of frustration with both my work and running, I had a business engagement in the suburbs east of Atlanta. A pedestrian trail system started right outside the hotel where I was staying. One afternoon, following a day of work where I felt like I had not communicated well, I contemplated a run. Thunderstorms were predicted, and the sky did hold some clouds, but planes were still landing and taking off nearby, so it had to be safe to run, right?

Once I started out, I almost immediately felt my body relax. The beauty of a run through a forest calmed both my physical and mental tensions. I reached a turnaround point overlooking an active beaver dam. I'd like to relate that the creatures showed me the light, but the beavers were napping or inside eating dinner. Even so, as I was heading back, I was enthralled by nature's bounty. A flowing creek, varied scenery, and the freedom of running without having to think about distracted drivers had me feeling better. Yet more was to come.

The sky opened, lighting struck far too close, and the ensuing rain was downright biblical. In places where I had to run uphill, the water rushed over the front of my shoes, drenching me to the ankles. I ran as quickly as I could and made it safely back to the hotel. As I stood under the awning at the building's entrance, I started to laugh. I laughed so hard and so long, that anyone seeing me would have thought I needed professional help. But, for the first time in many days, I felt alive. The funk was broken by the overwhelming power of nature.

Feeling trapped inside your head? Get out—but do check the weather radar first.

Sing It Out

I love music. In fact, I love music so much that, if given the awful choice of having to give up sight or hearing, I'd need a guide dog. Great music can sway my emotions, penetrate my moods, and make me glad to be alive. In fact, right now I have my "Resilience" playlist[7] streaming into my ears.

Most people have their favorite songs—music that prompts them to turn up the volume. I do too. However, sometimes hearing these tunes when I am in a funk feels like a cruel joke. I associate those songs with happiness, which is the opposite of how I feel. Even so, that might work for you. If so, crank up those faves. If not, find music that does.

A friend of mine recently suggested that music could be used as a tool for confidence. He recommended I find a song that I could listen to when friends or family were not available to boost my nerve for an upcoming event. He referred to this as a "battle song." Since music moves me anyway, I acted on the suggestion. I found a song that has the desired effect: "Rise" by Calum Scott.[8] That song is now a type of anthem for me. It does not get me hyped up; in fact, it does just the opposite. It calms my mind enough for me to think, Yeah, I do have "my best suit on" and "my sleeves rolled up" and "I'm ready." It nudges me toward hope and fosters a productive mindset.

The method can be applied in all sorts of circumstances. For example, Wanda felt down after a tough dance lesson. She could not master a new move quickly, and she felt like she was the only one who could not do it right. Back in her apartment, she instinctively hit the power button as she walked past her sound system. After a quick search on a music streaming service, she collapsed on the couch. She loved her chosen artist's lyrics and melodies, and she sang along with the first song.

Then the streaming service played tracks from the artist's newest album, a work Wanda had not yet heard. The lyrics seemed to speak directly to her. Song after song, the artist laid down a pathway out of the negativity Wanda felt. By the album's final track, Wanda was up on her feet, thinking through the move that had challenged her. After that she eagerly anticipated the next dance class. She also noted the name of the artist's new album so she could find it the next time she needed a melodic lift out of frustration and discouragement.

Find the music that stirs your soul and use it like a match when you need to ignite forward thinking.

Drop Expectations for Now

Do not go back to the source of a setback unless you do so without expectations. If a recent social interaction went awry, get with long-time friends simply to laugh together. If a work promotion eluded you, put your energy into the aspects of your job you most enjoy without concern for being recognized by your boss. Reconnecting with what drew you to the activity in the first place can ease your mind and allow you to enjoy it once again.

One way to reignite joy in an activity is to join a new group or club. For example, running with a group removes many of the pressures you have during serious training. It feels more social even though you are engaging in physical activity. A new group may also introduce you to new running routes, giving you a nice change of scenery. There are many factors of a group that can contribute to rediscovering joy in the activity.

The same is true of other activities. Feeling unenthused about your writing? Find a local writers club and join their conversations. Need a shot of motivation for building your photography portfolio? Find a photographers group and participate in their activities. You likely can find a club that focuses on your interest. Even if that group meets only online, the conversation can help you dig up the affection and motivation you know is there but not felt.

Yet solitude can work as well, as long as you don't put pressure on yourself. Jacob found himself studying the bristles of a paintbrush. Yesterday's work on a commissioned portrait had not gone well. A large black *X* was the last mark Jacob had made on the canvas. All his efforts to that point presented a stilted, unnatural result. Days of work, a moment of frustration, and a ruined canvas.

A glance across the room reminded him how much he loved painting landscapes. One of his latest artworks hung proudly on his studio wall. It was a painting he loved, both for the result and for the experience of painting it. Sitting on the hillside overlooking Valley Forge at sunrise had been an exhilarating and inspiring event. He grabbed a smaller canvas and headed outside. After a short hike, he found a flowing stream beautifully framed by the fall colors of water-side trees. He set up his portable stool and easel, opened his satchel, and spent several hours capturing the beauty he was witnessing. No expectations, no deadline, just the joy of painting.

The next day, Jacob returned to the commissioned work. (An artist has to eat!) The paint flowed from his brush in natural arcs, and by the end of the day, most of the portrait was complete.

Pursue nothing but joy in your endeavor, and you will find yourself becoming better at it. Let your passion guide you to resilience.

Learn Something New

Find a new way to interact with the world. Doing so may help you discover a direction pointing the way out of discouragement.

First, using your mental energies to learn something automatically engages your mind in labeling, sorting, pattern recognition, and application. These are the same cognitive processes that enable the making of meaning. By firing up your neural learning systems, you may discover better ways to revisit your setback.[9]

Second, learning something can provide you with new insights. For example, I once spent a few weeks taking drawing lessons. No, I did not become a world-class sketch artist in that brief time, but I did learn that drawing slows down my thinking, forces me to look at objects differently, and gives me another option besides words for thinking and communicating.

Adrianne had such an experience. On a whim, she registered for a martial arts class. She was surprised to find her first session mostly focused on vulnerabilities rather than moves. It was also enlightening to find the vulnerabilities were not physical. Repeatedly, the teacher stressed three areas: doubt, negligence, and skepticism. These, more than physical weakness or a lack of strategies and tactics, would determine a fight. On her drive home, recent conversations with editors came to Adrienne's mind. She had approached each one the same way: "Thank you for your time. I won't take much of it, I promise. Could you just look at my book proposal and tell me what needs to be improved?" She had projected doubt from the very beginning, as if she did not believe an editor would express an interest in her project. "Ugh," she uttered aloud. "I defeated myself with doubt."

Once home, she did some journaling. Writing out her thoughts made the problem obvious. Adrianne struggled with imposter syndrome—the feeling that even though she had successfully developed a book and a good proposal, she didn't feel like she had earned the right to be an author. Every editor knew immediately that she lacked confidence and assumed that the quality of her work was the likely cause.

The insight was beneficial. After her next meeting, an editor asked her to submit the complete manuscript. An insight gained while learning a new physical routine opened a path to potential.

Go ahead. Learn something new. It is one more avenue to insight.

Do for Others

Practicing the Golden Rule forces us to look beyond our own circumstances, and it frequently engages us in serving others whose circumstances are worse than our own. Meeting the needs of someone else helps us recognize our ability to influence the world around us. That includes our own lives.

During a season defined by injury, the local Parks & Recreation staff asked Sydney to develop and lead a "Couch to 30-mile" program for their members. She was low on motivation. Still, the opportunity to introduce people to cycling sounded like fun. Sydney soon had about a dozen people riding together on Tuesday nights. Week after week, she found herself more invested in each individual and more excited about the progress she saw. When race day finally came, Sydney stood at the finish line and watched every one of them cross it. She was more excited than when she crossed a finish line herself. Working with this group was fun. It was rewarding. It was motivating. A year later, Sydney rode her personal best in a challenging race. A year of training sparked, in part, by helping others accomplish their own goals.

Graham had a similar experience following a major blunder at work. He had led his landscaping team to the wrong address. Since the homeowner was not home, the team proceeded to do the yard work, hedge trimming, and some restructuring of the home's planting beds. When he got back to the office, his boss wanted to know why the team had not completed the assignment. The homeowner was waiting for the team to show up. Graham immediately felt sick. They had completed the requested services at the wrong place. Now, instead of one frustrated homeowner, there would be two. His boss sent him home for the rest of the day and told him to use the weekend to get over it. But Graham beat himself up and returned Monday morning still angry with himself.

His boss, recognizing Graham's frustration, gave him an easy assignment at an assisted-care facility. The teams that had done the landscaping there previously came back with stories of the residents' kindness, which often included lemonade and a chance to stand in the air conditioning for a few minutes.

Graham's team completed their work and were packing up their equipment when the social director approached them. She complimented their work and then said that several residents had been watching them through the windows and wanted to invite them in for a cool drink.

Graham and his team were treated like welcomed guests. In addition to fresh lemonade, cookies appeared, and soon sweaty landscapers and happy seniors were mingling and laughing. Graham felt good about the team's work, but he sensed that he had more, beyond manicured lawns and vibrant flower beds, to offer the residents. Before leaving, he talked to the social director about volunteer opportunities. He returned to the office with a new purpose.

Once a week, Graham visited the seniors he had met at the impromptu social. He played games with some of them, listened to their stories, and found himself laughing more—while there and at work. His boss noticed the change and asked Graham what was up. While explaining, Graham raised the possibility of the company becoming more involved, possibly launching an initiative focused on serving seniors. His boss liked the idea, seeing a good public relations move for the company. He put Graham in charge of the details.

Bringing his work and his volunteer worlds together created a fusion that enabled Graham's abilities to shine. Within a year, he rose from being a team leader to a management position focused on identifying and overseeing community service possibilities for the company.

Dealing with a setback? Find ways to serve others. Besides the better world you help create, you may find a path to better yourself.

Don't Be Idle

Whatever you do, don't let yourself become paralyzed by disappointment. When you don't fill your time, your thoughts will return again and again to the doldrums. The old adage "The idle mind is the devil's playground" has some truth to it. The more your mind heads in that direction, the more likely you are to either become depressed, give up on your goals, or both. Remember, you only fail when you quit trying. *Don't let yourself give up.* Find a way to process the feelings, move beyond them, and return to pursuing your goals.

When you are in an emotional funk, you need resilience on steroids. That may involve a break from activity, a change in activity, old friends who make you laugh, a new group of like-minded people, music or writing or talking, investing in others, or some combination of these suggestions. Make choices that create an environment where resilience can be found. *Choose* to uprise.

NOTE: Need help finding some music to stoke your resilience? Start with this Spotify playlist: https://open.spotify.com/playlist/759 t7DTXczUtEEWgjo92Eh?si=b3913502cb4245e1. Have a song that should be added? Contact me via https://www.kevindwashburn.com

PART THREE
INFLUENCE

CHAPTER 8

OTHERS

Examining the past enables improvement.
Considering the future sparks motivation.
These are the building blocks of strategy for the present.

66 **I** haven't really started yet. I mean, I have done some research, but I haven't started writing anything." Many teachers would have responded with some variant of "What do you mean you haven't written anything? The rough draft is due Friday!"

I was visiting a middle school in southern Alabama where I had been working with the faculty on effective writing instruction. The assignment, to write about a lesser-known individual who was involved in the Civil Rights Movement, seemed straightforward, but this middle school student was struggling. He hadn't written a single word. He hit a wall and could not figure out a way to get over it, and the clock was ticking. He needed to find resilience—not just for that day, but until a final version of his paper was complete.

What I witnessed over a few days in that classroom taught me much about how we can help others, including children, develop resilience. We'll return to observe this teacher throughout this chapter, but for now, let's explore why this matters.

We live in a world where anything "instant" and "easy" seems attractive. Hungry for fast food but don't want to leave the house? There's an app for that. Want your laundry detergent, a recent best-selling book, and a new USB adapter tomorrow? There's an app for that. Even if you want to find a date, there's an app for that! There is not an app for resilience.

We frequently celebrate but fail to cultivate resilience. We make heroes, at least for the moment, out of those who come back from devastating circumstances to reach pinnacles of accomplishment. You only need to watch a bit of Olympic TV coverage to know this is true. All this lionization of such individuals keeps them at a distance. We deceive ourselves into believing that we cannot be resilient like them.

We have seen that others can help us in times of need. So why shouldn't we do the same in reverse? Pass it on. Once you have cultivated the resilience to get back into the fight after a defeat, you can help others to become more resilient.

Back to the Future

We've explored the power of perspective in previous chapters. The nature of one's outlook can significantly influence resilience. So, part of helping others become more resilient involves helping them learn to redirect their viewpoints.

Humans are uniquely equipped to imagine a future and to work to make it a reality. Imagination fuels the initial effort and fosters resilience when challenges arise. Daniel Goleman explains that contemplating positive goals propels us forward. In contrast, thinking about weaknesses and struggles prompts a defensive response that is likely to diminish effort. "A conversation that starts with a person's dreams and hopes can lead to a learning path yielding that vision."[1] Resilience begins with a vision that says, "Here is what you can do!" before it emphasizes the step-by-step how-to of a process.

As a coach, I know this redirect is frequently needed. No matter how high an individual's fitness level may be, if he is pursuing a challenging goal, the training at some point will become difficult. A long run will get cut short, a speed workout will be slower than intended, or an "easy" run may suddenly feel difficult. Dismay and surrender are justifiable responses, but not ones that will move the runner forward.

As a choir director, I know mastering a challenging piece of music gets tough, even tedious at times. Parts have to be repeatedly reviewed. Cut-offs have to be simultaneous. Blending has to be practiced. I frequently "go back to the recording" when possible, so we collectively remember what the piece can be. To move forward, we need to look forward.

Let's examine how this plays out in that middle-school classroom. Remember, the student had not written a single word and the rough draft's due date was only days away. Here is how the conversation unfolded:

Teacher: How's your report coming?
Student: I haven't really started yet. I mean, I have done some research, but I haven't started writing anything.
Teacher: Okay. Who is the subject of your report?
Student: I thought I'd write about Reverend Robert Graetz.
Teacher: Tell me a bit about him.
Student: Well, he was Rosa Parks's neighbor. He led a church and supported the Montgomery bus boycott.

Teacher: Sounds like an interesting individual. You've already discovered some great details about him. Now, I want you to imagine someone you really respect reading your report. Do you have that person in mind?

Student: Yeah, I guess that would be my aunt. She teaches at the university.

Teacher: Great! Now, I want you to imagine that your aunt just read your report on Robert Graetz. She sets it down, looks at you, and tells you what she found most memorable about Robert Graetz. What does she say?

Student: Um, I guess she says, "Wow, what a courageous individual!"

Teacher: Excellent! So your writing really drew her attention to this man's courage. What events in Graetz's life did you write about that made your aunt think he was courageous?

Note the redirect here. At the beginning of the discussion, the student is lost, possibly overwhelmed, and likely spending mental energy on something other than writing. The teacher changes the direction of the student's thinking. She doesn't suggest the student "think harder" or exclaim, "I can't believe this is all you've gotten done!" Instead, she reorients the conversation. "Imagine the future," she suggests, and the student begins developing a vision for the writing—not just identifying who he wants to write about, but focusing on what to include and even how to structure the work. A glimpse at a possible future helps the student return to the work with a purpose.

This strategy is not just effective with school-age kids. It works with adults too. "Let's review our goals," I tell my runners. "When you imagine accomplishing one of them, what do you envision?" Imagining yourself crossing a finish line with a certain time displayed on the race clock is more motivational than fixating on recent work-out difficulties. Imagining the future can also help with adjusting strategies. Perhaps the recent speed workout was too aggressive for the current point in the training cycle. Maybe the date for a goal attempt needs to be moved back to allow more time for fitness to develop. That's not failure!

One way to help one another develop resilience is to call a time-out on current thinking. Negative thinking spirals downward, but future thinking propels upward. Encourage those around you to pause and contemplate what the future they are working for looks like, sounds like, smells like, feels like. The more senses you can bring into the vision, the more effective this future vision will be.

Such resets can help allay frustration. For example, Alicia reached a point with her sister that she wanted to call a time-out after every phone call. Each time she offered an idea for how to celebrate their parents' fiftieth wedding anniversary, her sister immediately responded with objections and unkind remarks. After each conversation, Alicia revisited every one of her sister's weaknesses and failures. As far back as childhood, Alicia convinced herself that her sister had always been against her. Mentally, she formed a script that she planned to use the next time they spoke by phone. She would unload all of it, hitting her sister with a detailed history that "proved" she had been Alicia's "enemy" from the start. Every negative thought ignited another until Alicia felt like she needed to make her mental list an actual list she could reference. She went searching for a sheet of paper and a pen when a different thought penetrated her self-righteous armor.

Back in their childhood, the sisters had taken some clapboards removed from their house when vinyl siding was installed. Together, they dragged a large section of connected boards into the nearby woods. There, they hoisted up one side of the panel, found sturdy branches to support it, and created a covered triangular space. A few old bed coverings later, they had a fully enclosed space with blanket "doors" on each side. They loved that space, eating lunch out there as often as possible, escaping there when they wanted time to talk, and using it as their own private space throughout their elementary school years.

Alicia picked up the phone and called her sister. "Do you remember our fort?"

"Huh?" replied her sister.

"That fort we made when Dad was putting siding up on the house. Do you remember it?"

"Oh yeah," said her sister, her voice revealing a slight smile.

Alicia talked about how much that fort had meant to her and how the time they spent together there formed a basket of memories she would cherish forever. Then she said, "Thank you for all those great memories."

Her sister paused a moment, and then asked, "Do you remember when we took the tube of chocolate chip cookie dough out there and shared the whole thing? We got so sick!" They both laughed.

Alicia took advantage of the truce. "You know, I always loved how much fun we had both in planning our schemes and in carrying them out. You always knew just how to make things work."

"And you were always brimming with ideas!" her sister exclaimed.

From there, the sisters shared, back and forth, things they appreciated about each other. A break in Alicia's negative thinking enabled a positive development. Ten minutes earlier, she'd been ready to deflate her sister with a list of negatives, further weaken the relationship, and concede all planning for the anniversary celebration. Now they were talking about what the anniversary commemoration could be. A shared vision emerged, and both looked forward to planning together and sharing the actual event.

When you sense someone—a friend, student, trainee, colleague, leader—is leaning toward giving up, help them envision the future. Call a time-out on the negative thinking, and reconnect them with what could be with continued effort.

Pausing in the Past

Reconnecting with a possible future does not guarantee that progress will never get bogged down along the way. At such times, revisiting how one has been working toward that future can be helpful. Let's see how the teacher we're observing used this in a later conversation with the same student.

> **Teacher:** Tell me about your writing so far.
> **Student:** I'm frustrated. I've got many isolated facts about Robert Graetz, but putting them into paragraphs—it's just not happening. Everything I write sounds choppy.
> **Teacher:** Okay, explain how you've been working on this.
> **Student:** Like I said, I've got a bunch of facts. I know I want to tell my reader that Graetz was a brave man, but I can only say that so many times before it sounds redundant.
> **Teacher:** Tell me about the facts you have.
> **Student:** Well, here's one. Because he supported the Montgomery bus boycott, his house was bombed three times.
> **Teacher:** Okay, that's a good fact. Tell me about the bombings.
> **Student:** That's all I have. Three times people who didn't agree with him tried to bomb his house.
> **Teacher:** So, you've got facts but not much context or detail for each one, right?
> **Student:** Yeah, I guess.
> **Teacher:** Okay, that doesn't seem to be working. Let's figure out how we can change your approach so that your writing com-

municates what you want. Let's begin with the facts. How could we find out more about the context of each one? If you were trying to tell me a story about Graetz's house being bombed, what would you, as the storyteller, need to know?

Student: I guess I'd need to have a beginning, middle, and end. Like I was writing a small story.

Teacher: That sounds good! So, if the fact that his house was bombed three times and he still worked for civil rights—if that shows your reader that he was courageous, we should tell those "small stories." How can we find the information we need?

Student: We could go back and see what our sources tell us about each of those bombings and try to come up with a beginning, middle, and end for each one.

Teacher: That sounds like a great plan.

While a glimpse of the future sparked the initial effort, at this point the student needs to reflect on the past so he can identify a way forward. The teacher, recognizing this, guides the student to think about how he has been working in order to think about a better way to proceed. Again, with the teacher's guidance, the student emerges from self-defeating thoughts and resumes moving forward.

Does this approach work with adults? Sadly, they are no more immune to wrong strategizing.

Take the surprise that backfired. Scott made a grand attempt to reconnect with his son and his family by showing up, unannounced—on Thanksgiving morning. He figured that making the long drive for a family holiday would communicate his strong desire to be among them. It would help make sure the past no longer mattered. When his daughter-in-law answered the door, she immediately called for

Braden, Scott's son. Braden came to the door, stepped outside, and pulled the door closed behind him.

"Dad, what are you doing here?"

"I'm here for Thanksgiving. I thought I would surprise you."

"I don't know what you are thinking, Dad. We haven't talked in a year, and now you just show up? We weren't expecting you, and we didn't plan on having anyone besides our family here today."

Scott did not miss what Braden implied. He was not thought of as family. And he was not welcome. He sighed and walked toward his car. Braden called out to him, but Scott kept going, entering the car and driving all the way back home.

"I just timed it wrong, I think," he explained as a friend, Jeff, listened. "The next time, I am going to show up but also bring the family an entire meal. That way there is no reason for us not to share a meal together."

"So," Jeff replied, "you intend to do the same thing, except with food this time?"

"Um, yes," Scott answered.

"Do you think that if you had showed up with food last time, Braden would have responded differently?"

"Hmm, I don't know."

"Let's say that this approach did not work for you last time. Agree?"

"Yes," Scott replied. "It was a disaster."

"Let's think about why. Maybe that will help us figure out a better approach for you."

Scott explained how the break in his relationship with Braden started, back when his son was attending medical school. Jeff continued asking questions until everything had been reviewed. At that point, Scott thought through what he had said.

"I know why it didn't work," Scott sighed. "It was basically the opposite of what caused our disagreement to start with. This all started because I didn't show up when I was supposed to at his White Coat ceremony. This time I showed up when I wasn't wanted, and I think Braden probably felt just as disrespected as he had back then."

Jeff nodded. "That seems like a probable explanation. So, since respect is at the core of the disagreement, what could you do differently when you try again?"

"I need to talk with Braden. Perhaps I could call him and see if he will meet me for lunch one day next week."

"I think that's a good idea," answered Jeff. "What will you do if he agrees?"

"I need to communicate my respect for him. He may need to hear me say that I am proud of him, that I recognize the incredible work it took to become a doctor, and that I made a mistake in not attending the ceremony. I need to fill the hole that my missing the ceremony created, at least as much as I can."

Jeff nodded. "That sounds like a great plan, Scott. I hope you can patch things up with Braden."

Scott's initial strategy did not work. Jeff helped Scott figure out why and how to change the strategy. Scott is now regularly invited to family events and holidays, and he never chooses to be elsewhere.

Yes, this approach works with adults.

Humans are, unfortunately, not automatically self-reflective. Like Scott, we like to "do," or at least feel like we are "doing." A pause to re-strategize is often forced on us through injury, a change in employment status, or some other dramatic—frequently negative—event. If we know when things are not working, why don't we stop and ask, "Why?"

What Jeff did is one way to help others: guide them through a series of thought prompts. First, for example, ask, "Regarding this challenge, what are you thinking right now?" Be sure you listen to and respect the response, but don't let the conversation end there.

Next, ask something like, "What could you tell yourself to redirect your energy?" Self-talk is one of the most powerful cognitive tools available. As sports psychologist Jim Afremow[2] explains, "thoughts determine feelings," and "feelings influence performance." Using self-talk effectively is an act of control. In the famous "marshmallow test," researchers asked the children who resisted eating a marshmallow right away what they did to withstand the temptation. Several indicated that they talked to themselves. They told themselves messages like, "You can do this. Try to wait for one more minute," and, "Imagine what else that thing could be besides a marshmallow." (An example of using self-talk to distract oneself!) The mind guides action, so if we can help someone regulate her thoughts, we can help her identify strategic actions.

Finally, ask, "What went wrong?" Or, as we explored in Chapter 3, "This strategy doesn't seem to be working. Let's figure out why so you can change your strategy and become successful." Help minimize the shame of examining a failure. Emphasize that it's the strategy, not the person, that isn't working. Then express your belief in the individual's eventual success. As you ask these questions, be sure to listen closely to the answers. They provide the information you need to ask the next one.

Let's see this work in action. Michael listened as empathetically as possible as Bryson detailed his work-related disappointments. While he had developed programs and materials that were highly respected within the company, adoption and sales of these products had been not as far-reaching as Bryson had hoped. He listed off a series of reasons he felt his ideas hadn't had wider influence. The marketing was poor. The potential clients were too lazy to try a program that didn't do all the work for them. Industry publications and event organizers were too cozy with larger companies. When he had exhausted his catalog of culprits, Michael stepped in.

"You obviously have a vision for what these products could do and how widely they should be considered. I understand your frustration at the pace of their adoption. Do you think about these disappointments a lot?"

"Well, I guess I do," sighed Bryson. "I just feel like my ideas have not gotten the audience they deserve."

"I understand. That is discouraging. In fact, I can't imagine that you feel good while focusing on them. Is there anything you could tell yourself in those moments that might help?"

"I don't know," Bryson said. "I get on a roll with the blame and have a hard time leaving it behind."

"Yeah, it's easy to do that. I mean, the frustration is always there, especially if you think about why it might exist. That's a lot of energy, though, that you are giving to thoughts that don't move you forward. Could you focus on something else to move past blaming?"

"Well, I still believe in those programs and materials. In fact, I've thought about new delivery options for the training parts of them. Thinking about potential ways to share them with a wider audience does inspire my creative, problem-solving mind."

"Wow, that's great," says Michael. "What didn't work about the ways you tried to share these ideas previously?"

As Bryson analyzed what hadn't worked—without stopping to assign blame—soon the conversation turned toward strategizing future efforts that might be successful. A good friend would have empathized with Bryson. A great friend helped him change his mental conversation and redirect his efforts. Looking back can help us find a way forward. Helping others look back can aid them in reaching their goals.

Redirecting the Present

A future hope and a look back have their desired effect when they influence the present. Taking action today gets us closer to a goal. How can we help others redirect their energies in the present? Let's return to the classroom and the teacher-student conversation. The student had suggested identifying a beginning, middle, and end to the attempted bombings of his subject's home, and his teacher agreed that this was worth trying. We pick up the conversation at that point:

> **Teacher:** That sounds like a great plan! Now, how will you go about coming up with that beginning, middle, and end?
>
> **Student:** I guess I'll just go back to my sources and see if they tell me anything else.
>
> **Teacher:** Okay, let's go back to the sources, but let's focus on one bombing for now. Is there one that you can recall any details about?
>
> **Student:** One of the bombs didn't go off, but it was the biggest.
>
> **Teacher:** Okay, let's start with that one. Find a beginning, middle, and end for the big bomb that didn't go off. Don't write anything that is untrue, but tell your readers the story and show them Robert Graetz being courageous. Focus on that one "small story" and write it. I'll check back with you to see how we can keep this moving. You've got a fascinating subject, and I think we've got a plan for how to show your readers his courage. Let's see what happens when you tell that one story.

The teacher brings the focus back to the present, guiding the student to recognize what the next step is and encouraging attention to just that step. The student can take the immediate action needed to make the imagined ending—the aunt responding to the writing—a reality without being overwhelmed by the entire process.

That is the key: helping others recognize the next step and supporting them in taking it. Feeling overwhelmed is deflating and often the initial step toward giving up.

When I am working with a runner who has a significant goal, such as one who wants to run her first full marathon, I give her only a few weeks of the training plan at a time. Extending a weekly longest run from seven miles to ten miles over a few weeks of time seems reachable. Usually, runners ask for the complete training plan, but unless they are experienced athletes, I resist that at first. The thought of extending a weekly run into the 20-mile range can be overwhelming, no matter how much time is planned between now and that step.

It helps to make such strategizing an invitation rather than an edict. This is especially true if you have to be the one delivering bad news. "Sugar coating" bad news sets up the brain for despair.

In the American South, where I live, we pile on the sugar. "Now, honey, I know you try really hard. Bless your heart. And I know your mama will not love you any less no matter what. I'm afraid I have some bad news. Before I tell you that, let me get you a sweet tea..." By the time we actually get to the "bad news," the brain is primed for an emotional overreaction. At that point, "the sympathetic nervous system kicks in, causing accelerated breathing, higher blood pressure, narrowed vision, and a cascade of physical reactions collectively known as the fight-or-flight response," which "overrides the higher-order thinking and invokes primal emotions that are beyond reason."[3] This is not a state in which an individual will respond strategically to feedback.

Here's what is more helpful. Be straightforward but offer the individual a choice. For example: "Your performance review for the last quarter suggests you need to develop better time management and

customer interaction skills. Would you like to review a couple strategies in each of these areas?"

By shifting the attention away from the bad news and onto a
choice to be made, you help the other person activate their prefrontal
cortex, a part of the brain that aids in regulating emotion and that
generates options for responses. In other words, you help the brain
stay out of the quicksand of despair.

What if you don't have an ongoing relationship with the person?
You may have to lay out the full plan, from now until the goal is
accomplished. However, help the individual identify clear bench-
marks or steps in the process. Depending on the process, it can be
helpful to add target dates to these steps. The key is to be specific
enough that the individual knows what to do. A goal is merely a vague
desire without a plan for what to do next.

Let's change the setting. You and your friend Parker encounter
one another at a school sporting event in the fall. Sometime during
the game...

> **Parker:** I really need to get into better physical shape. I've been
> telling myself that for a few months now.
> **You:** It's definitely challenging to do that with all the things we
> have going on. What's making it hard for you?
> **Parker:** I guess motivation right now. It's something I should
> do, but every time I think about it, I groan inside.
> **You:** I understand that. It's how I often feel about organiz-
> ing my office. I should do it, but I always seem to lack
> enough interest.
> **Parker:** Exactly.
> **You:** So, our kids are both playing spring sports too—about six
> months from now. If you started focusing on better health

tomorrow, how do you think I would respond after not seeing you between now and then?

Parker: I hope you'd say something like, "Wow, you look great! I can see how your work on diet and fitness is paying off!"

You: So, I'd be able to tell right away? Why? What do you think would be different about you? When you imagine yourself at that point, what do you see?

Parker: Hmm, a little less fat, a little more muscle, maybe even a healthy look on my face.

You: Think that's possible? Could you do it?

Parker: I know I could do it! In fact, I'm going to do it! You just wait until spring!

A glimpse of a possible future, and suddenly Parker is ready to make some changes. At the game the next weekend, you see Parker again...

You: How's it going? Were you able to start making your six-month vision a reality?

Parker: Well, I've started, but I have one stubborn challenge. I keep some snack items in the house for when the kids have friends over. Because I see those snacks when I open the pantry, it's tough to choose a banana over a bag of chips.

You: Yes, I can see why that is a challenge, and why that might not work. Let's think. Where else could you put those snacks? Do you have storage in your garage or your basement? If we change location of "Snack Central," I bet it will be easier for you to make good choices.

Parker: There are cabinets downstairs. I could store them there because I only need them when the kids have visitors.

You: That sounds like a good plan! Try it and let me know how it goes.

The current strategy isn't working. Let's look back and figure out why. Then let's change the strategy. Perfect!

Many people would just commiserate with Parker. Others would say, "Well you just need more self-control!" Judgment and discouragement rarely spark success. As a friend, you are cheering for Parker's success, so when he isn't moving in that direction, examining the past with an eye toward changing the present strategy is how you enable continued progress.

What if a friend, student, or colleague is the type whose emotions overrule their reason? Reasoned strategy is likely to go unheard and unheeded in that case. This could happen because of hastily voiced frustration by another colleague or superior, or, in the classroom, by some form of fear, such as test or math anxiety. Dr. Kate Beecher[4] offers some suggestions.

First, maintain eye contact, guide the individual's breathing while you breathe with him (e.g., in for four, out for four), and maintain a calm voice, speaking clearly with easy-to-follow directions for short steps. This can be done with an individual or group. For example, these strategies can help a class of students relax before taking a test, or a group of musicians preparing to perform.

Beecher also suggests engaging the mind to focus more on the moment. For example, asking the individual to name four things she "can see, hear and feel, then three more of each, then two, then one."[5] Connecting with sensory information in the moment helps steer the mind away from panic and toward a place where reason returns and strategic thinking is possible. A calm mind can strategize, but a panicked mind can only react.

Knowing Where to Point

Helping others find and develop resilience is a gift you can give over and over again. It is a selfless act—unless you are doing it hoping to be thanked or recognized in a future award acceptance speech. Not only does it support and encourage others, it helps us spread the influence of this positive character trait. It also increases the likelihood that you and I will find our own hope and resilience when we need it. If you have ten friends, and you help two of them become more resilient, you have increased the possibility of leaving interactions more hopeful than when you entered them by twenty percent—not a bad return for lending a listening ear, guiding with concrete suggestions, and experiencing excitement as you witness growth. You can help others develop minds primed for growth, performance, and achievement.

How do we point our friends in the right direction when they need to find resilience? Here are a few questions you can use to guide your own thinking:

- Is the individual struggling to get started? Does she know the goal but lack general direction or motivation? If so, help her envision a possible future.
- Has the individual started working toward the goal but reached a point where effort seems ineffective? Has what he has been doing failing to enable progress? Help him reflect on the past.
- Does the individual need to figure out what to do next? Does she need a strategy for action? Help her focus on the present.

Keep in mind that thinking in multiple directions may be necessary. For example, after reflecting on the past, a person needs a plan for what lies next—to move from the past to the present. Similarly, once a possible future has been envisioned, a person needs a plan for what to do now—to move from future to present.

Above all, be positive. What could be a more powerful gift to another person than your belief in their potential? Do not impose your own goal or strategy. Guide and suggest, but always let the other own the goal and plan. Remember, you may need help with resilience at some point. Supply the uprising lift you may need down the road.

NOTE: The teacher featured in this chapter uses the Writer's Stylus program, an instructional grammar and writing curriculum. The coaching strategies she applied are part of the training teachers receive in the Writer's Stylus Basic Course. For more information, visit https://www.writersstylus.com.

CONCLUSION

Resilience is accepting your new reality, even if it's less good than the one you had before. You can fight it, you can do nothing but scream about what you've lost, or you can accept that and try to put together something that's good.
— Elizabeth Edwards

His life began with a struggle for survival. In the small eastern African country of Eritrea, his mother collapsed from blood loss during the delivery and feared both she and the boy would die. He was born in the midst of a decades-long war between Eritrea and Ethiopia. At three months of age, his family escaped rising war violence in the city by resettling in the countryside. Once old enough, he spent much of his day foraging for wood.

Unfortunately, the war spread into rural areas. The boy's older brothers faced conscription into the Ethiopian army if caught. Russom, the boy's father, was also in danger due to his support of the Eritrean Liberation Front. Russom would prove to be a man of relentless resilience. When his wife was expecting their sixth child, he was forced to flee for his safety. The boy, his siblings, and their pregnant mother were now in less danger, but they also had to survive largely without the father's help.

Over the next seven days, Russom walked 225 miles to the border with Sudan. Though separated from his family, he held onto a hope for his children. He wanted each of them to have a world-class education. The circumstances must have made such a hope seem foolish to anyone else. In such conditions, most would consider educational opportunities to be a low priority. But Russom maintained a firm grip on his goal. His main obstacle was, in Eritrea, only one child per family was allowed to attend school. For any others, tuition would be required. When one of his older sons expressed no desire to go to school, Russom responded, "You don't understand the value of education. Once you do, you will blame me if I don't give you a chance."[1] Russom began looking for a way to provide the required tuition.

What characterizes such resilient individuals? What empowers their ability to uprise from adversity stronger? In other words, what did Russom have that enabled his resilience? Researchers have asked these questions and identified five traits[2] of those who do not stay down when knocked down.

The first of these characteristics is a survivor mentality. Resilient people do not see themselves as passengers in a car over which they have no control, but as drivers who can influence outcomes. They refuse to let defeat or failure be the final word, because there is something they can do. They choose to hold on to hope.

And a hope-filled mind can dream and scheme. It can imagine a better future and find the drive to plot a path forward. It continues to strategize and act while remaining alert to new moments of inspiration that flicker even when the pursuit stalls. Hope sees setbacks as temporary challenges. Being separated from his family by international borders and a seemingly endless war must have felt like a setback to Russom. Yet, even in these circumstances, he pursued his goal.

He found work and began sending money back to his family. That money, delivered by travelers going from Sudan to Eritrea, provided the tuition for the children old enough to start school. Still, it was not the type of education Russom hoped they would receive. Two students to each desk and three to each book meant that memorizing the teacher's lessons were the only means of "learning." And not knowing an answer could earn you a slap from the teacher or an older student. Definitely not the teaching techniques of a quality education.

For five years Russom continued to send as much money as possible from Sudan. Through the kindness of others and Russom's continued efforts, the family was finally reunited in Athens, Greece. When the young man who barely survived his own birth passed through immigration and ran to his father, Russom thought he was one of the younger children. The boy was so small and frail that Russom burst into tears. He was distraught by how sickly the entire family appeared.

At this point, it would have been easy for Russom to despair, to give up on his hopes for his children's education, and to blame himself for all the challenges they faced. They needed so much. They needed better nutrition. They needed a safe place to live. Russom had done his best, but perhaps it was not enough. If he had stayed with the family… or if he had made more money to send back to them… or if he had gotten them out of Eritrea sooner… So many ways he could have beaten himself up and surrendered his hopes. But that's not what resilient people do.

The second characteristic of resilient individuals is self-compassion. Resilient people give themselves grace for error. That does not mean they don't feel frustrated or discouraged. They do, but they do not let those feelings dictate their choices. They resist seeing themselves through their past shortcomings and maintain a view that looks ahead. Even though his initial reaction was despair, Russom let go of self-blame and kept pressing ahead. The past and his feelings about it would not be an excuse for giving up. Negative thinking would just spiral toward surrender.

From Athens, the family continued on to Italy. However, the children were not permitted to attend school there. They had escaped with their lives, but Russom's hope of an education for his children still could not be realized. He applied for the family to immigrate to the United States, but his application was rejected. Luckily, Sweden accepted the family's application. Hoping for more opportunities there, most of the family left Italy.

However, Russom had to stay behind in Italy after suffering injuries in a car accident. While recovering, he did not expect his family to return to him so quickly. Upon arriving in Sweden, Russom's wife and children were denied entry and detained in an immigration camp for a week. Then they were returned to Italy, where their first night back was spent in prison. Now what? They had fled a war-torn country, but Russom's hope seemed less logical with every rebuffed effort to move ahead.

Thanks to the efforts of the Red Cross, the children were able to attend a boarding school. A step forward, but still not the education Russom hoped for. A question kept bubbling up in his thinking: why had the United States rejected his family's application? In reviewing the paperwork that had been submitted, Russom discovered an error. The response to one of the questions implied that Russom had more than one wife. He immediately corrected the mistake, and then began cultivating allies. He sought the help of the Catholic Church, the Red Cross, and the U.S. Embassy in Rome. "His motivation to leave was to get us to a better educational system. He wanted to expedite everything because he didn't want us to miss out on another school year."[3] Although only these small steps were possible, Russom kept pushing for better solutions.

The third characteristic of resilient individuals is strong problem-solving skills. Even before an outcome is reached, resilient people are engaged in identifying challenges and strategizing effective responses. They do not accept a downward trajectory, such as a rejection by immigration officials or a car accident, as irrevocable. They look for an opportunity to reverse a trend, or a shift to a new goal that will lead to success. Resilient people do not cease looking for ways to prevail. They live by the motto that you only fail when you quit.

When the going gets tough, resilient people use their problem-solving skills to assess their current situation and address it. They find a strategy that will give them the grit they need. For Russom, education was a core value. When faced with the choice to move forward, step back, or maintain the status quo, Russom acted in accordance with the core value. While he was operating at the edge of what was possible, Russom finally reached a stage where he could ignite the efforts of those who could help him. He had done all he could, pushed ahead when challenges arose, but now he had to get others to apply their efforts in achieving his goal.

Additionally, his patience with the bureaucracy had reached its limit, so he communicated his sense of urgency. Red Cross workers listened as he described all that his family had gone through. He had the necessary documentation, he argued, so the family should be free to leave. Such impatience shown earlier in the process might have delayed or jeopardized the family's chances of immigrating to the U.S., but emotions never got the best of Russom. He governed his responses until a bit of demonstrated frustration could be beneficial. Just one week later, Russom, his wife, and his seven children landed in San Diego, California.

That is the fourth characteristic of resilient people. They regulate their emotions. They feel them like the rest of us, but they do not let their feelings go unexamined. They may feel discouraged after a setback or frustrated by an unexpected challenge, but they plan their way to healthier viewpoints, back to hope, and to renewed efforts. They do not let go of the idea that something good can happen.

Unfortunately, just getting out of one country and into another does not guarantee an immediately better situation. Russom's family still had plenty of challenges ahead of them. They still faced hardships on U.S. soil. The airline lost their luggage, so they entered the country with just the clothes on their backs. Low-income housing placed them in a neighborhood rife with challenges. At least the education Russom had hoped for could begin. Plus, new possibilities abounded in California. Russom and his wife got the children enrolled in schools as soon as possible. Because they needed to understand English to succeed in school, Russom began holding language lessons for his children before school every morning. Collaboratively, they gained the needed skills to understand and communicate in English. Even as they gained confidence in the language, they still were somewhat isolated.

Eritrean traditions kept the family celebrating together as the hard work of adapting to a new world continued. Eventually, they discovered others who, like them, had emigrated from Eritrea and shared their traditions. Although the difficulties had seemed endless, the family rose up as their community slowly grew.

The fifth characteristic of resilient people is they have strong social connections. They have people in their lives who leave them more hopeful. Don't isolate yourself from the support of a community. Even one person who leaves you more hopeful can be your greatest asset. For Russom's son who had a dramatic entrance into the world, a junior high gym teacher would be one such person.

A fitness test ignited a passion that would shape the boy's future. He always strived for an *A*, even in gym class. So, during a timed test, the young man raced around the school track, finishing the mile in 5:20. He earned the *A*, and his teacher encouraged his efforts on subsequent attempts at a faster finish. Meb had taken his first steps toward becoming one of the most beloved American runners in history.

The world took notice when Meb Keflezighi returned to Athens in 2004, the place where reuniting with his father had caused Russom such despair. This time Meb represented the United States in the Olympic Marathon. He won the silver medal.

Five years later, Meb was returning from an injury as he stood at the start of the 2009 New York City Marathon. As the elite runners took their marks, the commentators discussed several other runners, only noting that Meb was coming back from a serious injury. They obviously expected someone else to cross the finish line first. But hope—stubborn hope—combined with the resilience needed to come back from a setback, the mindset to learn from past failures, and the grit to persevere when the race got tough carried Meb to a first-place finish. What his father had demonstrated so often became part of Meb's character.

That would be enough, right? The Olympics! The New York City Marathon champion! No, not for Meb. Just as his father had, Meb kept pursuing possibilities. He challenged himself to continue.

In 2013, explosions near the finish line of the Boston Marathon triggered shockwaves throughout the running world and beyond. Cries of "Boston Strong" were heard in the months that followed. The city and the race demonstrated their own resilience, and America's oldest marathon took place again the next year. As usual, the elite runners were called to the start line first. The commentators mentioned Meb but suggested that perhaps his participation was symbolic. Someone else would likely cross the finish line first.

Once again, they were wrong. Meb Keflezighi, with the victims' names from the previous year's terrorism attack written on his bib, crossed the finish line first. From Eritrea to the pinnacle of his sport, Meb dared to hope and found a learning mindset, grit, and resilience when they were needed.

Meb is not the only one in his family who benefitted from his father's resilient determination. All of Meb's siblings attended universities, earning degrees in engineering, business, medicine, and law, among others. Hope, mindset, grit and resilience are a powerful set of tools, a gift that their parents passed on to them.

I've had the privilege of meeting Meb. At the expo of my first full marathon in Phoenix, Arizona, Meb was a featured speaker. (This took place in between his New York and Boston victories.) I asked him to sign my race bib, and he wrote "Run to win!"

I still have that bib. In fact, I'm inspired by it every day, since it hangs on a wall opposite my work desk. Not surprisingly, a man whose father overcame country borders to achieve his goal for his children and who has conquered so many of his own challenges titled his autobiography *Run to Overcome*.

Being resilient is seldom easy. But it is worth the effort. You can, intentionally, by applying these strategies, make advances toward achieving your goals. And if those goals remain out of reach, you will still be better off for the efforts you give. Build your resilience. Help others build theirs. That way, when we encounter one another, we can all take steps forward together.

Onward!

ACKNOWLEDGMENTS

L ooking back means directing your mind to what enabled you to pursue a worthy and meaningful goal. Specifically, to look back with gratitude. Who helped you along the way? Who has been there to cheer you on? Who has given you great advice along the way?

So many have helped, cheered, or advised as I've worked on this project—thanks to all!

Special thanks…

…to Julia. Having a wife who always encourages chasing ideas and interests is a gift. You inspire me through your own pursuits of creative expression. Thank you for just being you and for agreeing to be you with me. I love you. Let's at least double the time we've already had together!

…to Jim Evans, a friend, a mentor, and one of the most deeply thoughtful people I know. Jim, talking with you about anything, but especially writing, is always a joy. And a learning experience. You and Brenda are some of my favorite people on the planet. Your encouragement on this project motivated me to finish it.

...to Greg Stone, whose life influenced mine beyond my ability to communicate. Your humor, love for people, and competitive spirit still impact my life, and so many things I am today can be traced back to you. I miss you every day.

...to Jack Jacobs, my "running mate." Jack, when you read this book, I hope you discover how significant your influence on me has been, and how much I value your friendship. Congrats on being the "Local Legend" of Coker Park. (For now!)

...to all the runners I've coached, individually or as part of a group. I have and continue to learn more from you than I probably give. I still get a thrill watching you cross finish lines and achieve goals. Onward!

...to Scott Pope at 24e. Thanks for your inspiration, guidance, and occasional reality check. I hope you recognize some of our conversations in these pages.

...to Starbucks Pelham (AL). Thanks for preparing my ridiculously complicated latte and providing a space where writing is a joy. I hope to start another project soon so we can resume our regular morning meetings.

...to my friends who encouraged this project, advised on how to get it done, and helped me stay on track in its completion. I might have finished this project someday, but it would have been far in the future without your influence.

...to John Paine, editor extraordinaire. One reason I wanted to write a new book was for another opportunity to work with you. Thanks for your interest and expert guidance when I needed it.

...to the Nonfiction Group of Scriptoria 2022. You were an unexpected gift to me and to this project. You inspired me, advised me, and even supported me after our time together around a table. This book is better because of you, and I am a better writer because of you. May our paths cross again soon!

...finally, to you, reader. The greatest honor a writer receives is the reading of his work. Thanks for picking up this book. I hope it inspires and challenges you as much as writing it has me. May we all leave people more hopeful than than they were before meeting us.

REFERENCES

Introduction

1. Evans, James R. July 7, 2022. Personal communication.

Chapter 1

1. Doerksen, Brian. "Just Before the Silent Night," track 2 on *The Heart of Christmas,* Shining Rose Songs, 2019, AAC audio file.
2. Blacc, Aloe. "Here Today," track 4 on *Lift Your Spirit,* Aloe Blacc Recording, Inc. 2014, AAC audio file.

Chapter 2

1. Roosevelt, Theodore. 2015. "Roosevelt's 'The Man in the Arena.'" April 2015. https://www.mentalfloss.com/article/63389/roosevelts-man-arena
2. Williams, Kimberly Tinker. "Staying Power: A Multiple Case Study of Spirituality as a Factor of Resiliency in Female Public School Superintendents in the Southeastern Region of the United States." Ph.D. diss. University of Alabama at Birmingham, 2012.

3. Goodrem, Delta. "The Power," track 10 on *Bridge Over Troubled Dreams,* Sony Music Entertainment Australia, 2021, AAC audio file.

Chapter 3

1. Spadaro, Dave. 2018. "Inside The Game: How Players Do Film Study." January 28, 2018, https://www.philadelphiaeagles.com/news/inside-the-game-how-players-do-film-study-20309663.
2. Brooks, Robert. 2007. "Mindsets for School Success: Effective Educators and Resilient, Motivated Learners." Presentation at *Learning & the Brain: How to Shape the Developing Brain for Learning & Achievement,* Cambridge, MA.
3. Melore, Chris. 2020. "Having a Positive Outlook on Life can Prevent Memory Decline." October 2020, https://www.studyfinds.org/positive-outlook-memory-decline/.

Chapter 4

1. Stulberg, Brad. 2019a. "Our Best Advice on Performance and Wellbeing in 2019." December 2019, https://www.outsideonline.com/health/training-performance/brad-stulberg-performance-well-being-articles/.
2. Miller, Carol Adams. 2017. *Getting Grit: The Evidence-Based Approach to Cultivating Passion, Perseverance, and Purpose.* Boulder, CO: Sounds True, 4.
3. Ericsson, Anders & Pool, Robert. 2017. *Peak: Secrets from the New Science of Expertise.* New York: HarperCollins.
4. Turner, Cory. 2016. "Practice Makes Possible: What We Learn By Studying Amazing Kids." June 2016. https://www.npr.org/sections/ed/2016/06/01/479335421/practice-makes-possible-what-we-learn-by-studying-amazing-kids.

5. Stulberg, Brad & Magness, Steve. 2017. *Peak Performance: Elevate Your Game, Avoid Burnout, and Thrive with the New Science of Success.* New York: Rodale, 181-185.
6. Magness, Steve. 2015. "The Calm Conversation—How to Deal with Pain." January 2015. https://www.scienceofrunning.com/2015/01/the-calm-conversation-how-to-deal-with.html.
7. Stulberg, Brad. 2019b.
8. Hutchinson, Alex. "Inside Voice." *Outside* (July/August 2022), 38.
9. Chin, Jimmy in The Editors. 2016. "The Outside Questionnaire: Jimmy Chin." October 2016, https://www.outsideonline.com/health/training-performance/outside-questionnaire-jimmy-chin/.

Chapter 5

1. Sandberg, Sheryl in Stulberg, Brad. 2017. "Become More Resilient by Learning to Take Joy Seriously." April 2017. https://www.thecut.com/2017/04/become-more-resilient-by-learning-to-take-joy-seriously.html
1. Rocca, Mo. 2019. "Laura Branigan: Death of a Singer, Life of a Song." *Mobituaries with Mo Rocca,* Dec. 13, 2019. Podcast, MP3 audio, 44:00. https://podcasts.apple.com/us/podcast/mobituaries-with-mo-rocca/id1449045549?i=1000459494566

Chapter 6

1. Snyder, Brad. 2021. "Brad Snyder Is Always on the Move." April 2021. https://pressroom.toyota.com/brad-snyder-is-always-on-the-move/.
2. Snyder, Brad with Sileo, Tom. 2016. *Fire in My Eyes.* Boston: De Capo Press.

3. Barker, Eric. 2022. "How To Be Resilient: 5 Secrets To Mental Toughness (Pandemic Edition)." 2022. https://www.bakadesuyo.com/2020/04/be-resilient/.

4. Stulberg, Brad. 2016. "The Secret Link Between Gratitude and Performance. November 2016. https://www.outsideonline.com/health/training-performance/secret-link-between-gratitude-and-performance/.

5. Goodrem, Delta. 2012. *Bridge Over Troubled Dreams*. New York: Simon & Schuster.

6. Goodrem, Delta. 2020. "My Story Behind 'Paralyzed.'" August 16, 2020. https://www.youtube.com/watch?v=3yosCEmJiUk.

7. Jockers, David. 2022. "Stress Resilience: 12 Strategies to Grow Stronger Through Stress." 2022. https://drjockers.com/stress-resilience/.

8. Sandberg, Sheryl. in Stulberg, Brad. 2017. "Become More Resilient by Learning to Take Joy Seriously." April 2017, https://www.thecut.com/2017/04/become-more-resilient-by-learning-to-take-joy-seriously.html

Chapter 7

1. Coutu, Diane. 2017. "How Resilience Works," in *Emotional Intelligence: Resilience*. Boston: Harvard Business Review, 15.

2. Groopman, Jerome. 2005. *The Anatomy of Hope: How People Prevail in the Face of Illness*. New York: Random House, xiv.

3. Hendel, Hillary Jacobs & Fraga, Julie. "Anxiety Feels Terrible, But It Has an Upside. Here's How to Make It Work in Your Favor." *TIME Health* (Winter 2022), 22-23.

4. Mugerwa, Soul. & Holden, John D. 2012. "Writing Therapy: A New Tool for General Practice?" *British Journal of General Practice 62* (December 2012), 661–663.

5. Johnson, Kevin. "Smile When You're Learning." *Outside* (March/April 2022), 65.

6. Snyder, Brad. with Sileo, Tom. 2016. *Fire in My Eyes*. Boston: De Capo Press, 171-173.

7. Washburn, Kevin D. 2023. "Resilience," Spotify playlist: https://open.spotify.com/playlist/759t7DTXczUtEEWgjo 92Eh?si=b3913502cb4245e1.

8. Scott, Calum. "Rise," track 7 on *Bridges*, Capitol Records, 2022.

9. Washburn, Kevin D. 2011. *The Architecture of Learning: Designing Instruction for the Learning Brain*. Pelham, Alabama: Clerestory Press, 42.

Chapter 8

1. Goleman, Daniel. 2013. *Focus: The Hidden Driver of Excellence*. New York: HarperCollins, 173.

2. Afremow, Jim. 2013. *The Champion's Mind: How Great Athletes Think, Train, and Thrive*. New York: Rodale, Inc., 222.

3. Sohn, Emily. "Emergency Response for the Mind," *Outside* (November 2020), 62.

4. Sohn, Emily. "Emergency Response for the Mind," 62.

5. Ibid, 63.

Conclusion

1. Keflezighi, Meb. 2010. *Run to Overcome: The Inspiring Story of an American Champion's Long-distance Quest to Achieve a Big Dream*. Carol Stream, IL: Tyndall House Publishers, Inc., 14.

2. Cherry, Kendra. 2023. "What is Resilience? Characteristics of Resilient People." March 2023, https://www.verywellmind.com/characteristics-of-resilience-2795062.

3. Keflezighi, Meb. 2010. *Run to Overcome: The Inspiring Story of an American Champion's Long-distance Quest to Achieve a Big Dream*. Carol Stream, IL: Tyndall House Publishers, Inc., 26.

ABOUT THE AUTHOR

Kevin D. Washburn, Ed.D. is an inspiring runner, coach, and writer based in Pelham, Alabama. As the Executive Director of Clerestory Learning and Cofounder/Co-owner of Make Way for Books, Kevin's expertise extends far and wide. He wrote the influential Architecture of Learning instructional design model, the transformative Foundations & Frameworks instructional reading program, and the empowering Writer's Stylus instructional writing program. Kevin is also the author of *The Architecture of Learning: Designing Instruction for the Learning Brain*. From elementary to graduate classrooms, Kevin has dedicated himself to education and has coached numerous individuals to achieve their first 5Ks and beyond. Living with his talented wife, Julia, a fine art photographer, he finds joy in cycling, swimming, weight workouts, architecture, music, bookstores, and the captivating world of live theater.

A free ebook edition is available with the purchase of this book.

To claim your free ebook edition:

1. Visit MorganJamesBOGO.com
2. Sign your name CLEARLY in the space
3. Complete the form and submit a photo of the entire copyright page
4. You or your friend can download the ebook to your preferred device

A **FREE** ebook edition is available for you or a friend with the purchase of this print book.

CLEARLY SIGN YOUR NAME ABOVE

Instructions to claim your free ebook edition:
1. Visit MorganJamesBOGO.com
2. Sign your name CLEARLY in the space above
3. Complete the form and submit a photo of this entire page
4. You or your friend can download the ebook to your preferred device

Print & Digital Together Forever.

Snap a photo

Free ebook

Read anywhere